Solution-Focused Strategies for K–12 Leaders

Solution-Focused Strategies for K–12 Leaders provides K–12 principals, administrators, and district-level professionals with powerful, flexible strategies to build and sustain a school climate in which teachers and students co-construct solutions together. School leaders today face an intimidating variety of challenges, from teacher shortages and administrative overload to political battles and complex family relationships. Driven by the evidence-based Solution-Focused approach, this book will support practitioners in empowering students based on their personal hopes, strengths, and motivations instead of focusing on deficits and punishment. Intuitive instructions, real-world vignettes, and additional online resources further bring the book's tenets to life. With foundations in therapy, positive psychology, and school counseling, these broadly applicable response-to-intervention techniques will help education leaders to improve climate, develop teacher–student relationships, refine trauma-informed practices, manage conflicts with parents, and more.

Marcella D. Stark is Associate Professor of Counseling and the Counseling & Human Services Program Coordinator at Texas Christian University, USA, and a licensed professional counselor and supervisor (LPC-S) in the state of Texas.

Linda Metcalf is Professor of Graduate Counseling Programs at Texas Wesleyan University, USA, and a licensed marriage and family therapist and a certified school counselor. She is the creator and owner of Solution-Focused Schools Unlimited.

Also Available from Routledge
Eye On Education
(www.routledge.com/K-12)

The Playbook for Self-Directed Learning:
A Leader's Guide to School Transformation
and Student Agency
Tyler S. Thigpen, Caleb Collier, Amber Bryant,
and Brittney Toles

Cultivating Behavioral Change in K–12 Students:
Team-Based Intervention and Support Strategies
Marty Huitt and Gail Tolbert

Leadership for Safe Schools:
The Three Pillar Approach to Supporting Students'
Mental Health
Philip J. Lazarus and Michael L. Sulkowski

Harnessing Formative Data for K-12 Leaders:
Real-time Approaches to School Improvement
Stepan Mekhitarian

The Influential School Leader:
Inspiring Teachers, Students, and Families
Through Social and Organizational Psychology
Craig Murphy and John D'Auria

Solution-Focused Strategies for K–12 Leaders

Improving School Climate, Teacher Confidence, and Student Wellness

Edited by Marcella D. Stark
and Linda Metcalf

Routledge
Taylor & Francis Group
NEW YORK AND LONDON

Designed cover image: Getty Images

First published 2025
by Routledge
605 Third Avenue, New York, NY 10158

and by Routledge
4 Park Square, Milton Park, Abingdon, Oxon, OX14 4RN

Routledge is an imprint of the Taylor & Francis Group, an informa business

© 2025 selection and editorial matter, Marcella D. Stark and Linda Metcalf; individual chapters, the contributors

The right of Marcella D. Stark and Linda Metcalf to be identified as the authors of the editorial material, and of the authors for their individual chapters, has been asserted in accordance with sections 77 and 78 of the Copyright, Designs and Patents Act 1988.

All rights reserved. The purchase of this copyright material confers the right on the purchasing institution to photocopy pages which bear the photocopy icon and copyright line at the bottom of the page. No other parts of this book may be reprinted or reproduced or utilised in any form or by any electronic, mechanical, or other means, now known or hereafter invented, including photocopying and recording, or in any information storage or retrieval system, without permission in writing from the publishers.

Trademark notice: Product or corporate names may be trademarks or registered trademarks, and are used only for identification and explanation without intent to infringe.

ISBN: 978-1-032-73291-6 (hbk)
ISBN: 978-1-032-73033-2 (pbk)
ISBN: 978-1-003-46350-4 (ebk)

DOI: 10.4324/9781003463504

Typeset in Palatino
by KnowledgeWorks Global Ltd.

Contents

List of Contributors vii

1 **Introduction to the Solution-Focused Approach in Schools**...1
   Marcella D. Stark

2 **Facilitating Solution-Focused Meetings** 19
   Linda Metcalf

3 **Solution-Focused Strategies for Managing Conflict with Parents**...............................49
   Marcella D. Stark and Linda Metcalf

4 **Solution-Focused Teacher Supervision**................67
   Marcella D. Stark

5 **A Solution-Focused Approach to Trauma-Informed Practices** 83
   Denise J. Krause and Samantha P. Koury

6 **Lessening Frequent Flyer Student Returns and Student Discipline Referrals**....................109
   Linda Metcalf

7 **Working with Students in Crisis** 129
   Carol E. Buchholz Holland

8 **Successful Students with Autism and Intellectual Disabilities** 151
   Sharon Casey and Jennifer LeHuquet

9 **Involving Students and Families in Solution Building** 175
   Tara Gretton and Edwin Choy

10 **Exemplar: Strategies to Get Started in Your School** 199
   Xiao Ding, Jeeyeon Hong, Cynthia Franklin, and Linda Webb

Contributor Biographies

Carol E. Buchholz Holland, PhD, is an associate professor in the Counselor Education graduate program at North Dakota State University in Fargo, North Dakota, USA. She is a National Certified Counselor and a licensed school counselor. In addition, Carol is a fellow of the Oxford Symposium for School-Based Family Counseling, and the 2024 Solution Focused Brief Therapy Association President. She is also a former president of the North Dakota School Counselor Association and the North Dakota Association for Counselor Education and Supervision. She has presented internationally and throughout the United States on topics pertaining to the solution-focused approach.

Sharon Casey has a background in high school and adult education and considerable experience in organizations offering services to vulnerable populations. She has worked in educational settings with young people and adults who have personal and academic difficulties, in drug rehabilitation centers, and at one of Canada's largest suicide prevention centers. She has a master's degree in educational studies and a certificate in brief coaching from the Ontario Institute for Studies in Education (OISE) at the University of Toronto. She has been training practitioners in the solution-focused approach at non-profit community-based organizations, schools, and health agencies since 2018.

Edwin Choy is a certified Master Solution Focus Practitioner with the International Alliance of Solution-Focused Teaching Institutes (IASTI) and also a professional certified coach with the International Coaching Federation. Edwin's work involves training in solution-focused coaching for leaders, teachers, and parents. He has developed and facilitated a number of useful solution-focused trainings for educators in many Singapore schools. Edwin also co-founded the Centre for Fathering in Singapore to inspire dads to be more involved with their children which has impacted millions. He also appeared numerous times on the radio and at conferences. He has since been training fathers in many Asian countries.

Xiao Ding is a doctoral candidate at The University of Texas at Austin Steve Hicks School of Social Work and the recipient of the Michael R. Daley Endowed Presidential Scholarship for Doctoral Students. As a school social work researcher and practitioner, Xiao was trained to identify and assist high-needs children and families through evidence-based, culturally adapted prevention and early interventions. During her PhD training, Xiao gained knowledge and expertise in SFBT by continuously practicing as an LMSW and serving as an outside consultation staff member with Dr. Cynthia Franklin at the Gonzalo Garza Independence High School.

Cynthia Franklin, PhD, LCSW-S, LMFT, is the Stiernberg/Spencer Family Professor in Mental Health in the Steve Hicks School of Social Work at The University of Texas at Austin. Franklin holds faculty fellowships at the Humanities Institute and at the Meadows Center for Preventing Educational Risk in the Department of Special Education. She is an internationally recognized expert on solution-focused brief therapy (SFBT) and mental health. In the early 2000s, Franklin helped develop a solution-focused, dropout prevention program in Austin, Texas, Gonzalo Garza Independence High School, which has been recognized as a top five dropout prevention program from the U.S. Department of Education.

Tara Gretton is a Registered Social Worker and Accredited Solution-Focused Practitioner, coach, and trainer. Tara has over

20 years of experience working with adults, children, young people, and families within social care and education. Tara feels passionate about bringing the solution-focused approach into the everyday lives of school communities to support the well-being of staff, students, and their families.

Jeeyeon Hong, MSW, is a doctoral student at The University of Texas at Austin Steve Hicks School of Social Work. Jeeyeon has worked as a mental health therapist in both the United States and Korea, working with children and families from diverse cultural backgrounds. Jeeyeon's research interest is in implementing and evaluating Solution-Focused Brief Therapy (SFBT) for at-risk youth in school settings to address internalizing problem behaviors such as depression, anxiety, and suicidal ideation.

Samantha Koury, EdD, LMSW, is a co-director at the University at Buffalo School of Social Work's Institute on Trauma and Trauma-Informed Care, as well as a trainer and consultant on various projects. She is a graduate of the University of Buffalo School of Social Work and has a doctorate in educational leadership and organizational innovation from Marymount University. Samantha has over nine years of experience working with leaders, organizations, and systems to become more trauma-informed in their work. She is passionate about trauma-informed leadership, workforce wellness, and helping organizations and systems plan for, implement, and sustain trauma-informed change.

Denise J. Krause, MSSW, Columbia University. Ms. Krause is the Associate Dean for Community Engagement and Alumni Relations and Clinical Professor at the School of Social Work at the University at Buffalo, The State University of New York. She has been a contributing author and presenter for several peer-reviewed, solution focused, and trauma-informed publications and presentations. Ms. Krause has been involved in several ongoing teaching and training initiatives in New York since 2000. She regularly offers workshops and presentations on solution-focused practice and teaching at the university, community, national, and international levels.

Jennifer LeHuquet has 20 years of experience in administration and teaching. Currently the coordinator of complementary services for the Riverside School Board, she has also served as principal and vice-principal at a special-needs school and a large comprehensive high school with the English Montreal School Board in Montreal, Canada. Jennifer has a master's degree in educational leadership from McGill University and a background in science. She is the proud mother of two school-aged boys who have experienced challenges and triumphs in their education and who inspire her to continue to learn and lead with an open heart and open mind.

Linda Metcalf, MEd, PhD, LMFT, LPC, CSC, is a Professor of Graduate Counseling Programs at Texas Wesleyan University in Fort Worth, Texas, and a former middle school earth science and art teacher. She is the author of 11 books and the creator of the Solution-Focused Schools Unlimited podcast series and the Solution-Focused Connection, a free, biweekly webinar providing ideas for school counselors, teachers, and administrators. She has presented extensively in the United States, Australia, Japan, Newfoundland, Germany, Scotland, England, Norway, Amsterdam, Singapore, UK, Canada, Thailand, and more. She is Past President of both the Texas Association for Marriage and Family Therapy and the American Association for Marriage and Family Therapy.

Marcella Stark, PhD, LPC-S, is an Associate Professor of Counseling at Texas Christian University in Fort Worth, Texas, USA. She teaches in the Counseling & Human Services Program and serves as its Program Coordinator. Her research examines applications of the solution-focused approach, exploring its use in school administration, clinical supervision, student affairs work, and issues of political disagreement. Most recently, she spent a semester consulting with administrators in one school district, and those experiences informed this book. She has served on the board of the Solution Focused Brief Therapy Association in various roles including President.

Linda Webb, PhD, is an accomplished educational leader with over 30 years of experience in K-12 and higher education. She earned her PhD, master's, and bachelor's degrees from the University of Texas at Austin. Currently, she is the President of Red Shoe Educational Consulting. Linda has served as Principal of Garza High School and Senior Vice President of Education Initiatives at the Meadows Mental Health Policy Institute. An international speaker, she has shared expertise on solution-focused education worldwide. Recognized with honors like HEB Principal of the Year, she pioneered programs like Garza Online and advanced inclusive education initiatives.

Introduction to the Solution-Focused Approach in Schools

Marcella D. Stark

> I don't think you can be a good principal if you're not solution focused. I mean, I guess you could, but you probably wouldn't be respected. And you probably wouldn't stay in that position very long.
>
> – Elementary school principal

I have never met a principal who would deny being focused on solutions. So how is this approach different from every other approach used in educational settings? The answer lies in the recognition that finding solutions and problem-solving are two different activities. I recently spent a semester observing and consulting with educational administrators in one public school district. Specifically, I suggested how to manage various situations encountered by these educational leaders and noted the solution-focused strategies they were already using. Over the course of the semester, I observed teacher observation and feedback sessions; professional development gatherings; Individual Educational Plan (IEP) and Response to Intervention (RTI) meetings; bullying investigations; coverage of classroom, cafeteria, bus line, and after-school care; and many instances of soothing upset children, parents, and teachers. I was struck by how rushed their days were and noticed that they barely had time to breathe

DOI: 10.4324/9781003463504-1

(forget about a lunch break)! I consulted the National Center for O*NET Development (n.d.) to learn that there are 32 job tasks identified for K-12 education administrators (https://www.onetonline.org/link/summary/11-9032.00) and noted that I was regularly observing about nine of them. When did these administrators have time for the other 23? Of course, they certainly engaged in some of these additional tasks when I was not present, but what I witnessed would leave anyone exhausted. Many of these administrators reported spending a large amount of their time "putting out fires" or problem-solving, leaving them little time for analyzing data, creating plans, and developing partnerships.

Many educational leaders assume they are solution-focused because they are constantly looking for solutions to problems. Yet many of these same leaders spend an enormous amount of time talking about problems, which is antithetical to this approach. In traditional approaches to problem-solving, a medical model is employed: professionals diagnose a problem, learn all they can about the cause and symptoms, and eventually come up with a way to treat the problem. Educators using a medical model operate in the same way. For instance, when a teacher is struggling, it makes sense to find the reason for her struggle, right? The reason may be that the state has implemented too many restrictive standards. Perhaps she has too many students or she was not trained properly to integrate students from special education into her classroom. Or maybe she's just bad at classroom management? Or maybe it's a personality issue. Is she having trouble at home that is bleeding into her professional life? The list goes on and on. And yet none of these reasons point toward a solution. Such approaches carry a risk of making people feel worse instead of better. Have you ever noticed that the more time you spend talking about a problem, the bigger the problem gets and the more annoyed, angry, or defeated you feel?

Getting to the "why" appeared to be a question engrained in the school leaders that I observed. Don't get me wrong. Learning the "why" can be helpful. Learning why teachers continue to come to school every day and give it their all, learning why a student is more successful in one class over another, and learning why a parent believes a certain accommodation will result in their child's future success can be immensely helpful. It's focusing on the "why" of a problem that can end in futile, problem-focused conversations. Conversely, leaders who use a solution-focused approach spend their time examining what is working (even a little), times that the problem is less of a concern, and the strengths and resources of their staff and students. They ask questions such as:

- *What outcome are you hoping for? What difference will that make in how you do your job? What difference will it make for your students?*
- *Considering what you've already tried, what were the smallest things you noticed yourself doing that were helpful?*
- *How were you able to overcome this challenge? How were you able to stay calm and focused when things didn't go your way?*

The answers to these questions often contain creative solutions that will work best in the unique setting of the concerned party. Solution-focused conversations typically leave people feeling more empowered and hopeful. Isn't that what you want for your school?

Historical Foundations

The solution-focused approach began as an approach to family therapy. de Shazer et al. (1986) took a different approach to working with clients at the Brief Family Therapy Center, established in Milwaukee, Wisconsin in 1978. At that time (and currently), many approaches to counseling were based on theoretical models of what causes problems. Instead, these colleagues decided to focus on what works in therapy. Their team watched hours of therapy sessions from behind a one-way mirror and looked for conversations and processes that appeared beneficial to clients. Specifically, they examined what was it that the clients and therapists talked about that was helpful in bringing about positive change. From this investigation, they developed both language strategies and a way of thinking that are described later in this chapter.

Co-founder Steve de Shazer had received training at the Mental Research Institute in Palo Alto, California. He was influenced by their systems approach to brief therapy, as well as by Milton Erickson, a psychiatrist who focused on the strengths and resources that clients brought to find solutions to their problems (Lee, 2013). This attention to strengths is evident in the solution-focused approach. Like the teacher who looks for times when a student is behaving well in order to call attention and reward the good behavior, solution-focused leaders are always keeping an eye out for *instances of success* (George et al., 1999) or times when the problem is lessened. Time spent in conversation uncovering and exploring the "how" of these instances is more effective than time spent dissecting problems. When a teacher or student is able to identify what they are already doing to make positive gains, they are more likely to increase their use of those strategies to make success happen more frequently and in more situations.

de Shazer's partner and co-founder Insoo Kim Berg brought the solution-focused approach into the educational realm. Berg and Shilts (2005) developed a coaching program (Working on What Works or WOWW) to help teachers improve their teaching and relationships with students. Using solution-focused principles, a facilitator works with an entire classroom to empower teachers and their students to discuss what is already working in the class and to co-create goals that are important to them in their context (Wallace et al., 2020); teachers then continue to seek input from students and involve them in making decisions throughout the year. By seeking buy-in from even young students, the teacher is able to transform the culture of their classroom as everyone works together toward co-constructed goals.

Research Outcomes in Schools

Most of the research on the solution-focused approach in schools centers on WOWW. In the largest study on WOWW, Wallace et al. (2020) studied its effectiveness in 30 fourth and fifth grade classrooms, containing 30 teachers and 413 students; they discovered increased student attendance and improved teacher ratings of student performance. Other researchers have noted improved student behavior (e.g., listening skills, respect toward adults) (Brown et al., 2012); improved class relationships (e.g., working as a team, positive peer relationships) (Brown et al., 2012); and increased teacher self-efficacy related to creating a system for class management (Kelly & Bluestone-Miller, 2009), motivating students, and adjusting lessons to address the diverse student needs (Berzin et al., 2012). Wallace et al. noted that "All studies show that WOWW is well received by teachers and school leaders who are happy with the improvements achieved in the classroom" (p. 689).

Whereas WOWW is a program that involves entire classrooms, other research centers on the use of solution-focused brief therapy (SFBT) delivered by school counselors and school social workers in the form of individual or group counseling. These research studies indicate that SFBT may help students better manage the intensity of their feelings (Kim & Franklin, 2009), reduce behavior problems in the classroom (Franklin et al., 2008; Kim & Franklin, 2009; Vallaire-Thomas et al., 2011), improve academic performance (Fearrington et al., 2011; Newsome, 2004), and increase graduation rates (Franklin et al., 2007). Franklin et al. (2018) noted that SFBT interventions have successfully been utilized with various groups across diverse student populations and grade levels.

Flexible Approach for Use by Everyone

Solution-focused concepts may be used by school administrators, just as they are for school counselors and teachers, to create a positive and collaborative climate (Davis & Osborn, 1999).

Although it originated as an approach to therapy, it is now considered "an approach of useful practice techniques" (Korman et al., 2020, p. 47). Extending beyond the therapy room, the approach is used in schools, businesses, and medical settings (Shennan, 2014). Whereas counselors and social workers still refer to SFBT, many who use the approach refer to it as *solution-focused approach* or *solution-focused practice*. It may be used by anyone who engages in conversation to help another person find solutions to challenges and reach goals (Shennan, 2014). Therefore, it may be used by everyone who works in a school.

Throughout the United States, educational leaders follow an evidence-based framework for supporting students (as well as teachers and families) known as Positive Behavioral Interventions and Supports (PBIS). According to the Center on PBIS (n.d.), the use of PBIS has the potential to improve academic outcomes and social emotional competence in students, health and well-being in teachers, and the overall climate of schools. The PBIS framework offers three levels of support, including tier 1 systems and practices that are universal; they may be used by all to establish a positive foundation that enables the majority of students to experience success. Tier 1 interventions need to be easily implemented into normal school routines to be used consistently (Fazel et al., 2014). Because a solution-focused approach may be used by everyone in a school in everyday conversation, it provides ideal strategies for tier 1 interventions (Kim et al., 2017).

The last chapter in this book will discuss Garza Independence High School, a solution-focused school in Austin, Texas, where everyone in the school is trained in using a solution-focused approach. Not every school has the financial and personnel resources to reproduce such an environment as that described in the exemplar of Garza, but every school has the potential to become solution-focused. A principal's leadership style (and that of his or her leadership team) empowers and sets the tone for a school community (Hernandez, 2020), so it begins with you.

Solution-Focused Stance, Structure, and Strategies

Solution-Focused Mindset

So how do you become solution-focused? You begin with a collaborative stance that respects the expertise of your teachers, staff, parents, and students. Let's dissect that. Most administrators collaborate with others when possible, and yet there are times when they simply must make decisions independently. Solution-focused administrators will attempt to minimize the hierarchy as they seek multiple perspectives to inform their decisions. They regularly communicate with their leadership team, delegate responsibility to faculty and staff, and seek input from students, parents, and others in the community. When this is not possible, transparency may go a long way in encouraging future collaboration. For example, by sharing teacher evaluation rubrics, district policies, or the administrator's own priorities, an administrator demonstrates respect for others. Part of collaboration involves respecting another's expertise. I am not suggesting that parents or students are educational experts; I don't even suggest that every teacher is an expert in all education matters. Rather, this stance recognizes the expertise of each person on what they want and on their own experience—the teacher's experience in the classroom, the parent's experience raising a child, the student's experience at school.

Solution-focused practitioners refer to this as a *not knowing stance* (Anderson & Goolishian, 1992). Adopting this stance does not mean that the administrator knows nothing; it means that the administrator cannot possibly know the full experience of the teacher, staff, parent, or student with whom they are conversing. In order to collaboratively work toward solutions, the administrator must put judgments aside and listen with curiosity, all the while trusting that the person has a good reason for what they do. One administrator commented that it is sometimes difficult to trust that the person has the betterment of the child as a focus. But remember the not knowing stance—you don't know what the good reason is, only that the person has a good reason. Further, the person may define "betterment" differently than you do. Culture and experience color our perspectives, so even seemingly common words like "prepared" or phrases such as "a good day" have different meanings to different people. Curiosity is key!

The second part of the solution-focused mindset is a focus on strengths. When administrators are solution-focused, they are constantly on the lookout for what is working well. Many people describe this mindset as positive. Although it is true that solution-focused administrators focus on the positive, they do not engage in toxic positivity. As mentioned earlier, problems are validated but not dwelled on. Rather, they ask those around them what they want instead (of the problem/complaint), and they spend considerably more time considering how the strengths and talents of those in the school system may be utilized to find solutions. Of course, this consideration requires that the administrator first notice strengths and then explore details about how successes are achieved so that they may be replicated and expanded. When a leadership team compliments their staff, exploring these details is much more beneficial than a brief "good job" accolade, which may leave the individual believing the administrator does not truly appreciate the difficulty of a situation or what is required to achieve success (Ajmal & Ratner, 2020).

Structure of Solution-Focused Conversations

Administrators engage in numerous conversations throughout their days. Whereas some discussion takes place in a formal meeting, dialogue can take place in school hallways, parking lots, etc. and involve conversations that are five minutes or less. The structure of these conversations is the same:

> Step 1: Active listening to the person, paying particular attention to who and what is most important to the individual.

Step 2: Discover what the person wants, their *best hopes* (Ratner et al., 2012) for what will result from the conversation.

Step 2a: Explore *preferred future* (Iveson, 1994)—obtain a detailed description of their ideal result (e.g., confidence, better relationship). What will they notice, both about themselves and what is happening around them, in their preferred future?

Step 3: Look for instances of success. What is going well already that they don't want to change? When are times that the person's best hopes have been realized, even a little bit?

Step 4a: Task given or accepted. Discuss what you may do AND what a person may do.

Step 4b: When the hope is unreasonable or beyond the administrator's capacity to meet, explore what strengths and resources may be utilized to propel movement toward the person's hoped-for outcome.

Step 5: Request feedback and plan to follow up.

Solution-Focused Strategies

There are many solution-focused strategies that may be useful in each of the above steps, and they almost always come in the form of questions.

Identifying Preferred Future

Everyone has a preferred future or how they would like things to be. Learning what an individual really wants can save a lot of time, and there are a few different strategies for learning this information. The first strategy is the **best hopes question** referenced earlier. At the beginning of any meeting or conversation, ask the person about their best hopes for the conversation. What do they want to be different at the conclusion of your conversation? Focus on outcome rather than task. Often, individuals consider something specific that they want you to do rather than their preferred future, and they will often respond by giving you a task. For example, parents may answer the question by requesting that you move their child to another class. In such instances, it may be helpful to ask: *Suppose I were able to grant that request, what difference would that make for you/your class/your student?* or *How would that be helpful in …?* You may discover that what the parent really wants is for their child to have good relationships with the teacher and with classmates.

Another strategy for identifying a person's preferred future is asking a ***fast-forwarding question*** (O'Hanlon & Weiner-Davis, 1989) or a ***miracle question*** (de Shazer et al., 2007). Fast-forwarding questions are used to ask the person to imagine a point of time in the future (e.g., end of the school day, end of term) and to describe what will be different. An example is: *If we were to fast-forward to one month from now, what might be happening that would tell you that school is going better?* Fast-forwarding questions may be used in conjunction with the best hopes question—*If we were to fast-forward to the end of our conversation, what will tell you that it has been helpful and a good use of your time?* The miracle question serves a similar purpose and goes like this:

> Let me ask you a different kind of question about these. It's called the miracle question. Suppose that you go to bed as usual tonight, and while you're sleeping, a miracle happens. The miracle is that the problems you've been telling me about are solved! Only you're sleeping, and so you do not know right away that they've been solved. What do you suppose you would notice tomorrow morning that would be different—that would tell you, wow, things are really better!
>
> (De Jong & Berg, 2013, p. 14)

The miracle question may be adapted to fit the situation and person. For instance, a magic wand may be substituted for a miracle when working with younger children. Some practitioners prefer the traditional wording of "the problems you've been telling me about are solved", whereas others prefer to provide specifics given by the person (e.g., your child's grades are better, you have made a friend). Either way, be sure and tell them what the miracle is!

Which question you ask is often a matter of personal preference. You may find that one question works better in some situations. When the situation is a tangible goal (e.g., a high rating on the teacher evaluation rubric), you may prefer a fast-forwarding question. Conversely, when you suspect that the person's preferred future is a state of being (e.g., student coping well, new teacher feeling more confident), the miracle question may be preferable. With both questions, ask the person to walk you through that future or miracle day and paint you a picture, so to speak. You want to obtain as detailed a description as possible. You never know which detail may provide hints to a solution!

Scaling

Although solution-focused conversations begin with a focus on the future, solutions may be found in the present and past. A useful tool for exploring the present and past is the *scaling question* (De Jong & Berg, 2013). Using this tool, an administrator will ask the person to self-assess where they are in relation to the goal on a scale of 1–10, with 10 being the goal and 1 being the opposite. The goal may be a situation, characteristic, or motivation level; the possibilities are endless. Traditionally, the person's preferred future is 10. However, 10 does not need to mean perfection. In fact, you're making the conversation harder if it is perfection. Instead, it may be more helpful to label 10 as "good enough", where the person feels satisfied that the situation is improving and that they are hopeful of reaching an acceptable portion of their preferred future. Scaling serves a dual purpose of identifying *instances of success* (George et al., 1999) and setting tasks for movement toward the preferred future. With patience and persistence, you can usually help the person find an instance of success, also known as an exception to the problem or time when the problem was lessened.

Once the person has provided a number, keep in mind your curious, not knowing stance. Find out what the rating means to them. A 7 may be a high rating for some and a low rating for others. That said, if they give a rating of 1, you may wish to ask *coping questions* (Berg & Miller, 1992): *How are you able to show up for school each day and keep at it, in spite of these challenges?* Otherwise, you want to learn why they are not lower on the scale. What strategies have they used to get to that rating or to keep from falling lower on the scale? By exploring the lower end of the scale, you force the person to *self-compliment* (Berg & De Jong, 2005) or identify strengths and instances of success. The strengths and strategies identified may be helpful in finding solutions. Only after you have a good description of their rating (all the while keeping watch for strengths), ask them to describe the next higher number (or half-number). Have they ever been at a higher rating in the past? If so, what were they doing to make that happen (presume they played a role in that success). What will they notice when they've reached that higher rating? How will they know that things are improving? Their responses to these questions will help with setting tasks.

Tasks, Follow-up, and Feedback

Have you ever reached the end of a meeting or conversation and asked yourself, *"So what did we decide"*? A helpful practice for ending a meeting or conversation is to assign a task using elements of SMART goals (i.e., specific, measurable, achievable, relevant, and time bound). Before you begin envisioning worksheets similar to IEP plans, note that tasks do not have to be complicated. In fact, you want to set tasks that are easy to achieve. One task is to ask the person to look for times when their preferred future is happening, even a little bit, over the next week. This meets the SMART goals criteria because it is specific, the number of instances may be counted, it is within their control, it is relevant, and it is bound to a one-week time period. Be sure to follow up by either asking them to check back in with you or scheduling a time to check back in with you. The first is definitely easier! But when it is important, you may want to make a point to follow up yourself. If you're like most school administrators that I've met, you carry your phone with you. It just takes a few seconds to give yourself a reminder. Following up with students, teachers, parents, and other stakeholders goes a long way toward building a trusting, positive relationship.

Another way to build strong relationships is to ask for feedback. Just as it is important to follow up on tasks assigned or accepted, it's important to follow up on the person's best hope for the conversation. Revisit the person's best hope for the conversation. Was it met? When stakeholders leave conversations dissatisfied, they often bring up the problem again in the future in ways that demand more of your time and resources. By asking for feedback, you show the other person that you care about them, their concerns, and their relationship with you. With each relationship that you build, you are building a positive school climate.

Book Outline

It is my hope that this chapter has provided you with a reason to keep reading, as well as an introduction to the solution-focused approach that you may implement right away. If I was successful in motivating you to continue reading, you will find chapters that focus on various areas of your administrative role. The next three chapters will focus on your interactions with adult stakeholders—running meetings (e.g., 504, IEP), managing conflict with parents, and supervising teachers. By proactively involving these adults, you may reduce complaints and use them as resources to make your campus more solution-focused! Transitioning to students, there is a chapter on being trauma-informed, which affects adults and students alike. The subsequent three chapters focus on working with different types of students—your "frequent flyers" (i.e., the students who spend the most time in your office), students in crisis, and students with disabilities. The final two chapters provide exemplars of solution-focused schools. Chapter 9 provides examples of school programs abroad that have promoted buy-in from their students and families, and Chapter 10 presents a model of a solution-focused alternative high school in Austin, Texas. Both chapters provide strategies that you may implement on your own school campus. In each chapter of this book, you will find either a case study or a reproducible handout with specific steps or sentence stems to guide you in using the solution-focused approach in your work as a school administrator.

Are you ready to give the solution-focused approach a try? What?! You don't have time to sit down and read this entire book today? Well, below are some sentence stems to get you started. Put them next to your phone and computer, to guide you as prepare yourself to call a parent or respond to an email. Pick just one or two and try to work into some of the conversations that you have as you walk around your school.

- *What would you like to result from our meeting? What difference will that make for you/your class/your child?*
- *What has been going well?*
- *What do you like about your class/teacher/student?*
- *What might tell you that the situation is better? If things were starting to improve, what you notice?*
- *What have you already tried that has worked, even a little bit?*
- *I really appreciate that you .... How were you able to do that?*

References

Ajmal, Y., & Ratner, H. (2020). *Solution focused practice in schools: 80 ideas and strategies*. Routledge.

Anderson, H., & Goolishian, H. (1992). The client is the expert: A not-knowing approach to therapy. In S. McNamee & K. J. Gergen (Eds.), *Therapy as social construction* (pp. 2–39). Sage.

Berg, I. K., & Miller, S. (1992). *Working with the problem drinker*. Norton.

Berg, I. K., & De Jong, P. (2005). Engagement through complimenting. *Journal of Family Psychotherapy*, 16(1–2), 51–56. https://doi.org/10.1300/J085v16n01_11

Berg, I. K., & Shilts, L. (2005). *Classroom solutions: WOWW coaching*. Brief Family Therapy Center Press.

Berzin, S., O'Brien, K., & Tohn, S. (2012). Working on what works: A new model for collaboration. *School Social Work Journal*, 36(2), 15–26.

Brown, E. L., Powell, E., & Clark, A. (2012). Working on what works: Working with teachers to improve classroom behaviour and relationships. *Educational Psychology in Practice*, 28(1), 19–30. https://doi.org/10.1080/02667363.2011.639347

Center on PBIS (n.d.). *Why implement PBIS?* https://www.pbis.org/pbis/why-implement-pbis

Davis, T. E., & Osborn, C. J. (1999). The solution-focused school: An exceptional model. *NASSP Bulletin*, 83, 40–46.

De Jong, P., & Berg, I. K. (2013). *Interviewing for solutions* (4th ed.). Brooks/Cole.

de Shazer, S., Berg, I. K., Lipchik, E., Nunnally, E., Molnar, A., Gingerich, W., & Weiner-Davis, M. (1986). Brief therapy: Focused solution development. *Family Process*, 25(2), 207–221. https://doi.org/10.1111/j.1545-5300.1986.00207.x

de Shazer, S., Dolan, Y., Korman, H., Trepper, T., McCollum, E., & Berg, I. K. (2007). *More than miracles: The state of the art of solution-focused brief therapy*. Routledge.

Fazel, M., Hoagwood, K., Stephan, S., & Ford, T. (2014). Mental health interventions in schools 1: Mental health interventions in schools in high income countries. *Lancet Psychiatry*, 1(5), 377–387. https://doi.org/10.1016/S2215-0366(14)70312-8

Fearrington, J. Y., McCallum, R. S., & Skinner, C. H. (2011). Increasing math assignment completion using solution-focused brief counseling. *Education and Treatment of Children*, 34(1), 61–80. https://doi.org/10.1353/etc.2011.0005

Franklin, C., Moore, K., & Hopson, L. (2008). Effectiveness of solution-focused brief therapy in a school setting. *Children & Schools*, 30(1), 15–26. https://doi.org/10.1093/cs/30.1.15

Franklin, C., Streeter, C. L., Kim, J. S., & Tripodi, S. J. (2007). The effectiveness of a solution-focused, public alternative school for dropout prevention and retrieval. *Children & Schools, 29*(3), 133–144. https://doi.org/10.1093/cs/29.3.133

Franklin, C., Streeter, C. L., Webb, L., & Guz, S. (2018). *Solution focused brief therapy in alternative schools: Ensuring student success and preventing dropouts.* Routledge.

George, E., Iveson, C., & Ratner, H. (1999). *Problem to solution: Brief therapy with individuals and families* (Revised and expanded edition). Brief Therapy Press.

Hernandez, E. J. (2020). School prevention: How to increase student engagement. In B. A. Gerrard, M. J. Carter, & D. Ribera's (Eds.), *School-based family counseling: An interdisciplinary practitioner's guide* (pp. 258–282) Routledge. https://doi.org/10.4324/9781351029988-9

Iveson, C. (1994). *Preferred futures, exceptional pasts* [Conference presentation]. European Brief Therapy Association Conference, Stockholm, Sweden.

Kelly, M., & Bluestone-Miller, R. (2009). Working on what works (WOWW): Coaching teachers to do more of what's working. *Children & Schools, 31*, 35–38. https://doi.org/10.1093/cs/31.1.35

Kim, J., Kelly, M. S., & Franklin, C. (2017). *Solution-focused brief therapy in schools: A 360-degree view of the research and practice principals.* Oxford.

Kim, J. S., & Franklin, C. (2009). Solution-focused brief therapy in schools: A review of the outcome literature. *Children and Youth Services Review, 31*(4), 464–470. https://doi.org/10.1016/j.childyouth.2008.10.002

Korman, H. J., De Jong, P., & Smock Jordan, S. (2020). Steve de Shazer's theory development. *Journal of Solution Focused Practices, 4*(5), 47–70.

Lee, M. Y. (September, 2013). Solution-focused brief therapy. *Encyclopedia of Social Work.* https://doi.org/10.1093/acrefore/9780199975839.013.1039

National Center for O*NET Development (n.d.) *O*NET OnLine.* https://www.onetonline.org/link/summary/11-9032.00

Newsome, W. S. (2004). Solution-focused brief therapy groupwork with at-risk junior high school students: Enhancing the bottom line. *Research on Social Work Practice, 14*, 336–343. https://doi.org/10.1177/1049731503262134

O'Hanlon, W., & Weiner-Davis, M. (1989). *In search of solutions*. W.W. Norton.

Ratner, H., George, E., & Iveson, C. (2012). *Solution focused brief therapy: 100 key points and techniques*. Routledge.

Shennan, G. (2014). *Solution-focused practice: Effective communication to facilitate change* (2nd ed.). Red Globe Press.

Vallaire-Thomas, L., Hicks, J., & Growe, R. (2011). Solution-focused brief therapy: An interventional approach to improving negative student behaviors. *Journal of Instructional Psychology, 38*(4).

Wallace, L. B., Hai, A. H., & Franklin, C. (2020). An evaluation of working on what works (WOWW): A solution-focused intervention for schools. *Journal of Marital and Family Therapy, 46*(4), 687–700. https://doi.org/10.1111/jmft.12424

2

Facilitating Solution-Focused Meetings

Linda Metcalf

As a busy administrator, chances are that you are often asked to attend or chair meetings where topics or situations have escalated. You are often looked at as the decision maker, the wise one who knows just what to do. It is a pressure-filled role, especially when that meeting is only one of the many tasks you must deal with that day. As a result, your decisions may often require more time than you have, and as a result, you may rely on past experiences only. Those in the meeting are relieved that they do not have to brainstorm too much, as their lives as teachers are busy too. Everyone just wants to attend to a situation, get your feedback and suggestions, and move to the next issue. And they do move to the next and the next, and soon the names on the list are crossed off. Everyone leaves the room with a decision that affects a person, be it a teacher, student, or parent, without any input from them. When the plan does not work, the teacher, student, or parent can be described as "not motivated to change." This unfortunate conclusion is often due, in my opinion, to not involving them in the solution building in the first place. This problem-focused approach is the common approach in education today where noble and kind educators do their best to figure out what to do to solve issues yet fail. As a result, teachers become despondent, students continue to act as they did before, and administrators feel more pressure than ever.

But imagine not having to be that decision-making person anymore. Imagine, instead, being a solution-focused leader who simply provides a solution-focused process that brings everyone involved to the table, where everyone is responsible for change. This can happen more often when everyone decides on an outcome together. Just imagine how such a process could impact not only the lives of those discussed but your professional life as well.

This chapter will explain how a solution-focused approach can be utilized in faculty meetings and teams to gain compliance, engagement, and cooperation by not overindulging in problem-focused discussions. The chapter will also introduce "systems theory" (von Bertalanffy, 1950) that, when applied, can make a huge difference in the number of referrals you get each week. And finally, you will find that you can still embrace school policies, but in a manner that decreases conflict and creates compliance with those school policies, so you are no longer the bearer of bad news, but the bearer of hope.

More Than a Team Effort: Case Study

Eddie was a seventh-grade student who was constantly misbehaving in three of his six classes. No matter how often he was sent to the office with a referral, which typically resulted in a punishment, Eddie continued to misbehave. In fact, he often said, "I don't care," when the punishments got harsher. The administrator was exhausted and frustrated with Eddie, which resulted in harsh words that the administrator regretted every time Eddie left his office. Eddie was the oldest kid in his family, cared for by his grandparents who struggled to rear three school aged children while their daughter was in prison. Learning about the solution-focused approach seemed to be a way forward for the administrator, which led her to take a different stance one day when Eddie was referred again:

> Eddie, I have been wondering about something. Tell me, how is it that you behave well in your other three classes?

Eddie was quiet at first, but then he reported that in the other three classes where he behaved, the teachers seemed to like him. He said those teachers were cool and that he liked being in their classes because they were fun. The administrator was fascinated. She asked Eddie what those teachers did that let him know they liked him, and what they did that made class fun. Eddie said that they often asked him to help them with things, which never happened in the other classes, and they occasionally told him that he did a good job. They also never yelled at him, he said. If he "messed up," they just sat down with him and talked to him after class. He said one teacher often had lunch with him in the cafeteria to talk about cars. The administrator then asked Eddie an important question:

> *So, as a result of those teachers asking you to help them and saying you did a good job sometimes, making it fun, talking things out with you when you messed up (Eddie's words) and ate lunch with you sometimes, how did you behave for them?*

Eddie stretched in his chair and smiled and said, I'm good.

The administrator asked Eddie if he would like to come to the eighth-grade team meeting that week as her "guest," where each of Eddie's teachers would be attending. Eddie wasn't sure about that and said if the other three teachers were there, it would probably not go well for him, since he was in trouble in their classes so much. The administrator promised Eddie that she would not let anyone say or do anything to upset him.

Then she said there was something she wanted Eddie to do for the next few days, like an experiment. She asked Eddie to pull up a chair in her office to her computer, where she wrote an email to all of Eddie's teachers. The email went like this:

Dear Teachers,
On Friday, at our eighth-grade team meeting, Eddie Haskell will be attending as my guest. Until then, please notice five times in your classes when Eddie does well. (He highlighted the word, "well.") *Write down details of those times and bring your notes to the meeting.*

Thanks,
Ms. Carter, Administrator

On Friday, Eddie showed up to the team meeting, but he was asked to sit outside for a short time while the administrator got the meeting started. Eddie seemed to be quite nervous!

The administrator began the meeting with the teachers by saying that the team meeting was going to be conducted differently on that day. She asked everyone present what their best hopes were for Eddie. Several teachers talked defiantly about what Eddie did wrong and needed to stop, while others talked about their best hopes being that he would be successful and gain something out of their classes ... that they saw him as a good kid in a tough situation. The administrator asked those who complained:

So, what might Eddie be doing someday instead of that?

That question stumped a few teachers, who tried responding the same, but the administrator kept asking, "and what would be better?" until they gave an answer of a better outcome such as what he would be doing. The administrator was patient and waited in silence at times, knowing that if she stepped in too quickly to rescue those slow thinkers, she would rob them of solution building later.

After the group members answered the *best hopes question*, the administrator shared with the team that she had learned that in three of Eddie's classes, Eddie did well and was never referred to her office. She looked at the teachers of those classes and smiled. She curiously asked them about what they did that worked with Eddie, and they responded. She then shared that when she asked Eddie to describe what went on in those classes, he told her. She then shared briefly what Eddie said. The room began to get quiet at that point. The teachers who were constant referrers of Eddie sat back a bit perplexed and slightly aggravated that their peers had success and they did not. Yet the administrator continued to talk about the successful classrooms, asking the successful teacher, "what else did you do?" and "how did Eddie react when you did that?"

After a few more responses, the administrator had what she needed to invite Eddie into the meeting. Everyone was surprised to see Eddie walk in. He was quiet as the administrator asked Eddie to sit near her, a strategy she often used to help the student feel comfortable and supported in a room full of adults. She had also asked Eddie's grandparent to attend that day, who chose to sit in the back of the room and listen. She then told the teachers, in front of Eddie, that she was impressed with how he behaved well in some of his classes. Eddie began to smile but looked down. He couldn't recall ever attending a meeting with the administrator like that. At that point, the administrator again read to all the teachers what Eddie had told her worked in those classes. There was little discussion after that.

I will share what happened with Eddie toward the end of this chapter. But until then, imagine how different this *solution-focused team meeting* might be from the last one you held for a student who was constantly in your office. Perhaps you had his parents present, or an irate teacher who was ready to transfer him into another class or suggest he attend another school. Perhaps the student was anxious and angry that he was again singled out and referred. That would be a scenario that is more common these days, as 62% of schools continue to promote zero tolerance policies (Perera & Diliberti, 2023) and enforce again and again, without success, punitive ways of trying to gain control. Unfortunately for millions of school children, the problem-focused approach is not helpful in today's schools. Be it the pandemic effects, family life, poverty, and marginalizing factors, problem talk is leading to … more problems.

Solution-Focused Team Meetings Are Systemic!

When I was a school counselor, I learned a lesson from an extraordinary administrator that I have never forgotten. As a solution-focused school counselor, I met with countless students each day dealing with all sorts of issues. Once the student felt better and came up with a plan, I would sign their pass and send them back to class. But then I started noticing the same students coming back too often. I was perplexed and thought: "how is it that they were fine when they left?" Then one day, it dawned on me what was happening. I knew the importance of thinking *systemically* (i.e., thinking of how problems are maintained and orchestrated through interactions). I had overlooked the importance of including the teacher in the plan. When my administrator sat down with me for a midterm review, he talked favorably about how I worked and then said at the end:

> *Some advice, Linda. When you see a student in your office referred by a teacher, never send them back to that teacher that day. Keep them in your office. The teachers are still angry and that causes the student to act up again.*

From that day on, I recognized the importance of always including the teacher in the plan when working to help a student make changes. Schools are *systems* (Metcalf, 2021, pp. 169–173), meaning that they are composed of many moving parts, such as teachers, counselors, administrators, and parents. Rarely do those moving parts come together to talk and focus on an outcome, where they develop a task together and agree to do their part in implementing and maintaining the desired change. I learned to walk the student back to class *every time* the student wanted to make a change in the classroom, knock on the door of the classroom, and invite the teacher out for a 30-second chat that went like this:

> *Ms. Harvey, thank you for referring Eddie to me. I want you to know that I work for you as much as I do Eddie. He and I have talked, and he has come up with some new ideas to show you the student he wants to be. Would you mind watching him, just today, for what he tries? I will then come by tomorrow and check out what's going better. Eddie – go show Ms. Harvey who you are!*

The first few times I did this, some teachers were at first annoyed, and that resulted in my adding, "I work for you as much as I do for Eddie." Then, they typically stopped frowning and something miraculous began happening. The students did not return much at all! I did follow up the next day and asked, "What's going better?" Notice, I did not ask, "How are things going?" That question can result in a complaint. As a result, the teacher and student were more likely to focus on what was working.

Teachers rely on you for solutions, and you probably know all too well the stress that causes you, which keeps you from being as effective as you want in other areas of your job. That dependence upon you also pushes you into an isolated conversation with a student without knowing or experiencing the dynamics of the system. In other words, you only hear the outraged teacher. You don't know about the other six hours of the day, which may be rich with *instances of success*, or times when the student does slightly better. That leaves you at a loss and unfortunately guarantees that you and Eddie will see each other again soon. But by involving the *system* of the student, you are much more likely to hear from everyone what needs to happen to create a solution. In other words, you may begin to see that it was the inner workings of the system itself that created the problem, not just one person. The solution then becomes changing the interactions, which only the system can do.

Therefore, a solution-focused team meeting involves the entire system. You can even invite the social worker, the cafeteria worker, the parent, the grandparent, or anyone in the child's system. With more interactions that include not only the complaint but also instances of success, you are more likely to have incredible, new, and proven ideas on the table to try. And here's the exciting part ... the student is present for the later part of the meeting, primarily so they do not hear the negativity that can often occur. Then, imagine being a student who feels that his teachers do not like him, sitting in a room with up to nine adults, where six of those adults are talking about his attributes, not his attitude.

Watching what happens to a student like Eddie at the end of a solution-focused team meeting is one of the most exciting experiences I have had when working in schools. I literally watch the relationships among everyone in the room transform from dislike and frustration to collaboration. As for the student, you see the attitude shift, the frown disappears, and motivation sets in. To date, after a solution-focused team meeting for behavioral referrals, I rarely saw that student again for the same offense. The system took charge.

Leading the Solution-Focused Team Meeting

If you recall from the case study early in this chapter, the administrator did not immediately take Eddie to the Friday team meeting. If she had, she might have found teachers who were surprised to see Eddie, and he might have heard more criticism. Instead, the administrator talked to Eddie regarding what was different in the classes where he behaved well. She noted his responses and asked him if she could have his permission to share with all his teachers what seemed to help him behave. She then prepared for the meeting by sending Worksheet 2.1 to all the teachers and asked that they watch for times when Eddie did slightly better.

It is important to email Worksheet 2.1 with high importance to everyone in the student's system, so it is no surprise that the focus will be more on possibilities rather than problems when the meeting begins. This will make a big difference as everyone begins to brainstorm what they want versus what they do not want.

Worksheet 2.1
Instances of Success Observations

Dear Teacher,

There will be a solution-focused conversation for _____, on _____ in room _____ at _____ o'clock. Your presence is requested because you are an important member in the student's academic life. The meeting will not last longer than 30 minutes.

Prior to the meeting, please notice times when this student is slightly successful in your classroom. Note the kinds of lessons, activities, behavioral interventions, motivational strategies, or other methods that help the student to be slightly more successful. Please list at least five of those times below and bring the list to the meeting.

Thank you,

_____

Times, situations, activity, when the student was slightly more successful:

1. _____
2. _____
3. _____
4. _____
5. _____

(Metcalf, 2010, p. 72)

Once the meeting starts, ask the student to wait outside the meeting room while you begin the meeting. This is a safeguard in case some teachers are so upset that they continue to complain and share their frustrations. From there, it will be important to listen to your faculty and gradually help them focus on what they want to occur instead of what they do not want to occur. Use Worksheet 2.2 here, as it will provide a template for you to use and guide the meeting toward solutions. Remember, the best hopes question gives you direction, or an outcome to achieve. Make sure to write down everyone's best hopes once they express them specifically in a future-oriented fashion.

©Linda Metcalf, 2025

Worksheet 2.2
Solution-Focused Team Meeting

Date: _____

Student: _____ Grade: _____

Primary Teacher: _____

Team Members: _____

_____

_____

Parent: _____ Administrator: _____

1. Identify the best hopes of everyone present:

"What are your best hopes for our meeting today in regard to our student _____?"

_____

_____

_____

_____

"On a scale of 1–10, with 1 meaning the student is not successful at this time and a 10 meaning the student has achieved success, where is the student?"

Parent: _____

Student: _____

Teachers: _____ (average score)

2. Create the preferred future for the student, together:

"What will the student be doing in the classroom (or other context at school) over the next three weeks so that the score increases and our concern decreases? Let's be very specific, with action-oriented answers":

_____

_____

_____

3. Discover instances of success:

"Teachers, would you please review your 'Instances of Success Observation' sheet and share with us the times when you noticed the student doing slightly better?"

_____

_____

_____

"Parent(s), could you please share with us the times when things have gone better in other classrooms, grades or even situations outside of school for your son/daughter?"

_____

_____

_____

4. Create a plan, based on the instances of success for the classroom, home, or curriculum:

Classroom:

_____

_____

_____

Home:

_____
_____
_____

Curriculum:

_____
_____
_____

Summary:

"What did everyone find helpful, if anything, as we talked today?"

_____
_____
_____

Next meeting date: _____ Time: _____

(Metcalf, 2010, pp. 73–74)

©Linda Metcalf, 2025

Copyright material from Marcella D. Stark and Linda Metcalf (eds.) (2025), *Solution-Focused Strategies for K–12 Leaders*, Routledge

Once you have found out what everyone's best hopes are, you can begin asking teachers about the *instances of success* they wrote down on Worksheet 2.1. That will begin to empower you and them with ready-made solutions since the instances of success have occurred already. It is important to listen carefully to the teachers as they share times of slight success. Make notes on what you hear worked with the student and ask questions to identify specific actions that worked. Make sure everyone contributes. The beauty of the meeting is that while several teachers will readily share their instances of success, other teachers who thought that they did not have success may begin to recognize instances of success as well. It is peer pressure at its best!

At this point, invite the student and parent into the meeting. Read back both lists—the best hopes list and the instances of success list. Ask the student if he would like to comment on what helped him achieve the instances of successes that you mentioned. If he is too shy to answer (and that happens a lot), continue asking the teachers what they think they did that helped the successes to happen. Asking these questions with curiosity empowers and compliments your teachers, and you will see them gradually relax and appreciate your focus. Add the comments to the second list. The student at this point will be starstruck, listening to teachers who the student felt disliked him talk about slight successes. It is this element at its core that will boost your chances of success.

The next section in the solution-focused team meeting process is *creating the preferred future*, which is what everyone, including the student, wants to occur for the student in the future. Make sure everyone contributes, especially the parent, student, and yourself. Please go slow on this section as the descriptions need to be rich and full of details. The dialogue below shows the importance of inquiring consistently:

Admin: What will Eddie be doing that will tell you things are better in the near future?
Teacher: He will be passing my class.

Admin to Student: What might you be doing that will show your teacher that you can pass?

Student: I will need to do my work and stay in my seat.

Admin to Student: How would your teacher know you were doing your work?

Student: I guess I would be sitting there at the computer putting in the answers and not talking to Stan.

Admin to Student: What might your teacher be doing?

Student: Maybe come ask me if I understand it.

Admin to Teacher: Could we try that, Ms. Harvey, just for this week, where you ask him if he understands the assignment, as long as he does his work and stays in his seat?

Teacher: I can try that.

Admin to Teacher: Thanks. I wonder, Ms. Harvey, what difference it might make for you when Eddie does begin to pass your class.

Teacher: Honestly, it would feel really good. I have tried to reach him but just could not seem to get there. I would really feel great to see him succeed. I have a lot of students and knowing he was working to pass would be great.

Do not worry if the student does not know what to say. Continue asking other teachers to express what they would see. The important part of the preferred future is that the student is no longer hearing problem talk. He is hearing solution building from everyone in the room. Imagine how different this conversation would be to the student, now that people are wanting to make changes for his benefit. See how these questions connect teacher and student? I also like to ask the student what their *teacher* might do to help them be successful. Once answered, you can then ask the student what he is willing to do more of when the teacher tries out his suggestion. This is a respectful way to align you with the teacher and the student.

At the end of the teacher conversation, ask the parent:

Admin: So, Grandmother, what might it do for you when Eddie is more successful at school?

Grandparent: I wouldn't worry so much about him. Then, I might be able to work a little later in the afternoon and be able to buy him more things that I know he loves. I would be happier.
Admin: Eddie, did you realize that doing slightly better in school could impact your grandmother that much?

Most students do not realize the extent of how their behavior and actions affect other people. That is why I like administrators to ask teachers what difference it would make when the student begins to succeed. Students need to hear their impact on others, such as the teacher and the grandparent. It also works in other ways if a parent is exhausted from trying to reach their child and help him succeed. By asking them "What is the impact of being called so often from the school?" in front of the student, the student then begins to see the impact he is creating. Then, you can jump into creating a preferred future with: "So, let's imagine that things begin to get better for you, Dad, and you aren't getting so many calls from school. How might that affect you?" Most parents are quick to look at their child and tell them straight how much better their lives would be. As for the child, they begin to understand slightly better that their changing can affect others.

At this point in the meeting, pass out Worksheet 2.3, which is simply a reminder to teachers to meet with the student once per week and discuss what went well. Show the student what the sheet looks like. Remind your teachers to ask the student what they did to bring out the student's success. Ask the teachers to review Worksheet 2.3 with the student on Friday, each week. Explain that by highlighting when things went better, they both begin to understand what created the preferred future that benefited them both. At this point, look at the student and encourage him to show his teachers the student he can be.

Worksheet 2.3
Student Successes

Date: _____ Student: _____

Teacher: _____

Week 1:

1._____

2._____

3._____

4._____

5._____

Score: _____

Week 2:

1._____

2._____

3._____

4._____

5._____

Score: _____

Week 3:

1._____

2._____

3._____

Copyright material from Marcella D. Stark and Linda Metcalf (eds.) (2025), *Solution-Focused Strategies for K–12 Leaders*, Routledge

4._____

5._____

Score: _____

©Linda Metcalf, 2025

Before ending this section, I want to troubleshoot a bit. While most solution-focused team meetings go well, such as the one described in this chapter, there will be times when a concern is so tough and teachers are so burned out that conducting one as smoothly as the one described may be challenging. This is what is referred to as "resistance," and it will happen. What to do? Stay the course! Yes, never be tempted to jump in and take over and make decisions for your team, no matter how unhappy or unwilling they may be to look toward an outcome rather than complain, because if you do, you will be (a) blamed if it does not work and (b) asked again to help on the same issue. But what is vital when resistance does appear is that you see it as a signal that what you are asking staff to do is not their goal. That means you must turn to them and say:

So, it seems we are at a standstill here. I must not be focusing on what you want. Let's talk more about how you want things to be for YOU.

You see, while we all want to create the best climate for students, unless your teachers get to focus on the preferred future that impacts them better, there will be resistance. Help the teachers achieve what *they* want, and you help students. That means if the teachers say: "What we want is for Louisa to be expelled so we can teach." Then, you say, "So, if Louisa would be expelled, tell me what difference that would make for you." This response sends a message that the teachers are heard. Then listen and write down their answers and say this:

I see how important it is. Tell me about times when you are able to ____ (whatever their answers were) just slightly, when Louisa was in the classroom.

Notice the language. "Tell me times" is different than asking "Has there been a time?" Then, listen to what they tell you, and from there, begin to brainstorm with them how more of that can begin to happen, as a team. You may be quite surprised at what they come up with.

Again, to troubleshoot when the meeting may not go as smoothly, keep in mind that this is a very different approach to solution building than what your teachers are used to. If needed, do not hesitate to say:

> *Everyone, it seems we are having a little trouble identifying times when things have gone better for Eddie. Let's try and watch over the next week, until our next meeting, times when things go slightly better for Eddie. I look forward to hearing from everyone when we meet again. Teachers, please write down what you see. And, Eddie, I would like you to help by showing your teachers some behaviors that show them that you know what to do. Can we agree on this, everyone?*

Meet again the following week and review the answers to Worksheet 2.3 with everyone present. Worksheet 2.3 is simply your blueprint for what is working and what to continue doing.

The Solution-Focused Faculty Meeting

I once provided solution-focused training for a Midwest school district that was struggling with too many referrals to special education. The district had decided to take on a solution-focused approach so teachers could begin focusing on competencies of students, not deficits. As a result, the referrals slowed, and teachers, although reluctant at first, became incredibly adept at noticing instances of success. As a result, the special education referrals dropped dramatically. While the school administrator watched the teachers begin changing their approach in the classroom, he was concerned about keeping the momentum going. He knew how often new initiatives failed, even when they were initially successful, so he decided to facilitate solution-focused faculty meetings.

He began by asking the faculty for agenda items a week before the faculty meeting each month and then he added his. This contribution seemed to be received well, as he often was overwhelmed with requests! But he kept them on the agenda. Before the meeting began each time, he did something extraordinary. He would walk through the hallways and notice what seemed to be working in classrooms. He watched teacher interactions with students in the hallways and during lunch. As he began the meeting, he talked about his observations and thanked the faculty, saying how proud he was to be there with them. For items that were concerns, he utilized the following guiding questions:

1. *Best Hopes: So, tell me, what are your best hopes regarding this issue?*
2. *Instances of Success: Tell me times when the issue is not occurring as much?*
3. *Preferred Future: What will it look like when this issue is not occurring as much?*

He then put the teachers to work. They began talking about the differences it might make for them at school and about how that would affect the students. He asked:

So, on a scale of 1–10, with a 10 meaning we are there, successfully dealing with this issue, where are we now?

This made the teachers think of where they were and most of the time it led them to realize that they weren't in such dire straits. If they said they were at a "4," the administrator asked:

So, what would it take for us to work together and get to a 5?

He put them back into groups to brainstorm actions to move up the scale. When they came back together, the solutions to move up the scale were written on a whiteboard. Together, the faculty agreed what to try to slowly move up the scale.

What was great about this meeting was that the administrator obtained "buy-in" by letting the staff map out what they wanted. There's always buy-in when people are working toward what is meaningful to them. There was a catch, however, that would keep them accountable. The administrator would hold another brief faculty meeting two weeks later to check in on what's going better. He would also remind his faculty that he would be watching for differences due to their efforts. He also planned a celebration of some kind after six weeks of effort. The faculty responded positively. Because they chose the concern to discuss and the strategies to move up the scale, they were more invested in trying something new. The team leaders who met each week were to remind the faculty about the project. They also adopted the solution-focused approach, when the administrator met with them separately and talked about the importance of seeking solutions rather than focusing on problems. The administrator gave the Solution-Focused Team Meeting template (see Worksheet 2.2) to team leaders and let them know that he wanted them to use it. It was such systemic applications to a variety of situations that helped the administrator's school in the Midwest to continue to lower and keep low, special education referrals, which eventually led the district to be in compliance.

Conversations with Students and Parents

The helpfulness of the solution-focused approach lies in its collaborative nature and simplicity. As you have seen so far in this book, almost any situation can be addressed using the approach since the approach is not about applying predetermined recipe-type strategies to specific situations. Instead, every situation is unique and so will be the solutions. When students and parents come to talk to you, the same format from the team meeting can be used. Here again are steps to take. First, greet the person(s) and put aside your agenda. Instead, start the conversation as follows:

1. Begin with the question: *What are your best hopes for our time today?*

   Ask this of all individuals who are in your office. Asking everyone makes the meeting collaborative and helps everyone to feel heard. Again, make sure the best hopes answers are clear and action oriented. Do not worry if the best hopes are unreasonable or impossible. Instead, ask what having an unreasonable or impossible outcome would do for them. Keep asking what difference it would make until you get to an outcome that everyone can address. Here's an example:

   > A teenager once told me his best hopes would be that his dad was alive again. I gave him my condolences and then asked how having dad around again might be helpful. He told me that his dad was the only person who supported him as a gay male. His dad also believed in him and helped him with science projects since his dad was a doctor. By this conversation, I was later able to ask sensitively, "so, it seems your dad gave you what you needed when he did this. Tell me, who else in your life now can give you a fraction of what dad gave you regarding these ideas?" The teenager talked of his uncle, who supported him and a neighbor who is a science teacher. We then had a place to start.

2. Ask about instances of success: *Tell me times when things have gone better for you and ____ happened slightly.* Again, see how the question is worded. Write down the instances of success when a student has stayed at school for two or three weeks without being referred to the office. Ask how the

student was different at home or in school to make that happen. Ask the parent for times in the past when their child did not get in trouble at school as often.
3. Co-create the preferred future with the following questions:

> *Suppose, when we end our conversation today and you (student) go back to class, and your mom goes back to work, and somehow, things get better here at school.*
>
> *What might your teachers notice about you just for this afternoon? As a result of that, how might things be at home?*
>
> *Write down the plan. Share the plan with the student's teachers. They are the system who must be informed to participate in the solution building, and it will help them to see the student differently and respond better.*

4. Follow up with the student the next day! Consider it to be a break from sitting in your office, if you ever have a chance to sit! Go find the student, ask for him to step into the hallway, and say, simply, "Tell me what's going better today?" No need to discuss the issue. Just listen. If at first the student does not know, let the student know that you will check back the next day.

Summary

Before ending this chapter, I promised to share what happened to Eddie after the meeting with his teachers! At the end of the meeting, something remarkable happened to Eddie as he sat listening to all his teachers. The teachers who had success with him in class naturally came over to him and gave him a hug, telling him how proud they were that he was so polite in the meeting. Following them, the other teachers who had not had such luck also came over to him, and I overheard the following from a few of them:

- *I am willing to try my best, Eddie, if you will try your best.*
- *Eddie, I am sorry that I did not know to come ask you if you understood an assignment. I will do that.*
- *Let's try together, okay?*

Eddie was floored at the responses. He looked at the administrator and his grandmother when everyone left and told the administrator that he had never had a meeting like that one. When asked if he liked it, he said, "Yes, it was really cool."

Eddie's principal checked on him for a few days that week and thereafter did not check anymore, as Eddie did well. He began getting involved in school activities at the encouragement of some of his teachers. His grades went up, and according to his teachers, he became a successful student by the end of the school year.

3. Always involve the person(s) in conflict with your office or meeting together, so you can guide them into solution building with each other.
4. Listen well, yet avoid asking about the problem and why it occurs.
5. Remember to give the student a chance to describe to you personally, what they need from teachers, and ask the student to share it in the meeting.
6. Your faculty members and your students are experts on their own lives. Inviting them to work together increases success immensely.
7. When you do not know where to turn or how to respond, that is the time when you need all the players in a current dilemma in your office to get direction for a preferred future.
8. When there is resistance, it is usually because the goal addressed is not important enough to those who are involved. To find compliance, find out what is important to everyone, then you can progress.
9. If someone gives you an impossible best hopes answer, go with it by asking "what difference would that make for you?" Ask the same question over and over until you get to an outcome that can be addressed.
10. Remember that people typically want things that they have experienced before. Thus, instances of success are gold.

References

Metcalf, L. (2010). *Solution focused RTI – A positive and personalized approach to response to intervention* (p. 72). Jossey-Bass Teacher.

Metcalf, L. (2021). *Counseling toward solutions – A practical, solution-focused program for working with students, teachers and parents.* Routledge.

Sentence Stems for the Solution-Focused Team Meeting (Reproducible)

I know this is a tough situation. Let's begin by di[scussing what every]one's best hopes are.

> *I realize that this student has been a challenge [to] me, how have you made it through the past [?]*
> *Tell me times when this student is slightly better[.]*
> *Thanks for telling me what is going on. What [are your best hopes] for our time?*
> *What might the student say YOU did on days [when he is] slightly better?*
> *I realize that this student has created a tough situ[ation. Tell] me times in your careers where you were dea[ling with a] challenging student, and you found a way to [help? What] else did you do?* (repeat)
> To the student: *Tell me, on the day when you w[ere better,] what did you do that might have made a dif[ference?] What did your teacher do?*
> To teachers: *Tell me how things will be for you p[ersonally when] the student begins to do slightly better in class.*
> To the parent: *Tell me what difference it will mak[e when] your child/adolescent begins to do slightly bette[r.]*

Chapter Tips for Administrators

1. It is not necessary for you to have all the ans[wers.] by not having answers and expecting othe[rs to figure] things out, you give them a better chance to [experience] competency and success.
2. Think systemically. When a student shares w[hat a] teacher did that made a difference, ask the stu[dent if he] can share that discovery with all his teachers.

Sentence Stems for the Solution-Focused Team Meeting (Reproducible)

I know this is a tough situation. Let's begin by discussing what everyone's best hopes are.

> *I realize that this student has been a challenge to many of you. Tell me, how have you made it through the past few weeks so far?*
> *Tell me times when this student is slightly better in your classrooms.*
> *Thanks for telling me what is going on. What are your best hopes for our time?*
> *What might the student say YOU did on days when he was doing slightly better?*
> *I realize that this student has created a tough situation for you. Tell me times in your careers where you were dealing with another challenging student, and you found a way to engage her. What else did you do?* (repeat)
> To the student: *Tell me, on the day when you were doing better, what did you do that might have made a difference for you? What did your teacher do?*
> To teachers: *Tell me how things will be for you personally, when the student begins to do slightly better in class.*
> To the parent: *Tell me what difference it will make for you when your child/adolescent begins to do slightly better in school.*

Chapter Tips for Administrators

1. It is not necessary for you to have all the answers. In fact, by not having answers and expecting others to figure things out, you give them a better chance to experience competency and success.
2. Think systemically. When a student shares what another teacher did that made a difference, ask the student if you can share that discovery with all his teachers.

3. Always involve the person(s) in conflict with your office or meeting together, so you can guide them into solution building with each other.
4. Listen well, yet avoid asking about the problem and why it occurs.
5. Remember to give the student a chance to describe to you personally, what they need from teachers, and ask the student to share it in the meeting.
6. Your faculty members and your students are experts on their own lives. Inviting them to work together increases success immensely.
7. When you do not know where to turn or how to respond, that is the time when you need all the players in a current dilemma in your office to get direction for a preferred future.
8. When there is resistance, it is usually because the goal addressed is not important enough to those who are involved. To find compliance, find out what is important to everyone, then you can progress.
9. If someone gives you an impossible best hopes answer, go with it by asking "what difference would that make for you?" Ask the same question over and over until you get to an outcome that can be addressed.
10. Remember that people typically want things that they have experienced before. Thus, instances of success are gold.

References

Metcalf, L. (2010). *Solution focused RTI – A positive and personalized approach to response to intervention* (p. 72). Jossey-Bass Teacher.

Metcalf, L. (2021). *Counseling toward solutions – A practical, solution-focused program for working with students, teachers and parents.* Routledge.

Perera, R. M., & Diliberti, M. K. (2023). *Survey: Understanding how U.S. public schools approach school discipline.* Brookings. https://www.brookings.edu/articles/survey

von Bertalanffy, L. (1950). An outline of general system theory. *British Journal for the Philosophy of Science, I*, 134–165.

3

Solution-Focused Strategies for Managing Conflict with Parents

Marcella D. Stark and Linda Metcalf

A school administrator is often juggling planning, substituting in classes when teachers need a break or must be absent, conducting a bullying investigation, and calming down a student who was having a meltdown in the hall. This administrator manages these various duties with grace and ease, but they are often filled with a sense of dread upon receiving a message that a parent wants to meet with them. Parents might send an email, but they very rarely request a meeting just to tell you what a great job you're doing. The first step in preparing for a parent-requested meeting is to prepare your mindset.

Seeing Parents as a Resource Rather than a Thorn in Your Side

Years ago, I (LM) was being interviewed for a director's position where I would use my marriage and family therapy background in schools, helping students by inviting their parents for conversations. The interview went well and one of the last questions asked of me was:

> So, what will you do with demanding parents, who want things done that are impossible to do?

I quickly responded:

> *I will first of all not think of them as demanding. I will think of them as passionate about seeking success for their child or adolescent. They did, after all, agree to meet with me, taking time out of their day to do so.*

I got the job. Afterward, the superintendent said that my remark about parents being passionate was different than how others answered the same question. He was intrigued that perhaps there was another option for working with parents other than just telling them they had to follow policy.

There are many ways to conceptualize how to work with parents who seek your time. One way is to see them as a thorn in your side, ready for a battle in your office, or as resources to tap into for improving your school. How administrators think of parents (especially demanding ones) has a lot to do with their mindset which can set the stage for solution building and a constructive conversation. Although district rules and guidelines must be followed, it has been the experience of the authors that solely focusing on rules and guidelines can alienate parents and send them off thinking that the school indeed does not like their child. Alternatively, Franklin et al. (2018) suggest that parent meetings can afford "an opportunity for the parent to shift from a position of frustration or defense to a position of feeling like a partner who can help bring about change" (p. 113). Instead of taking a top-down, problem-focused approach and being ready to tell parents why what they are asking can't happen, solution-focused administrators are able to lessen resistance by considering the parent's request as something important to them. Taking on a mindset where you consider that they took the time to come to school and talk to you can help you to greet them as a partner and develop a conversation that pleases everyone. The solution-focused conversation strategies in this chapter will help you do that.

Solution-Focused Strategies for Managing Conflict

Once you have prepared yourself to take on a new mindset and be solution-focused in a parent meeting, it is important to have a single question on your mind—*What does this parent want?* Before diving into this question, it is important to build a friendly, positive, and collaborative relationship. Consider beginning the conversation with something different—ask what they appreciate about their student. You may have every intention of avoiding a conversation consisting of complaints and demands, but it can happen very quickly. To avoid a problem-filled conversation, it is important to begin with strengths—is the student passionate, funny, or kind? Starting with the student's strengths serves to lessen tension, provide the parent to reminisce fondly about their child, and remind you both "why" you are in the meeting. It also places you in the position of collaborator rather than adversary. Beginning this way also gives you a glimpse into what the parent values most, which will help later in building solutions together.

First Look for What Is Going Well
Based on the response you receive from the parent about why they requested the conversation, there are two options for further creating a positive dialogue. One option is to adopt a presumptive stance that there are some things going well for their child at school and ask what they might be. You may say something like:

> *What is going well right now for your child at school that we can build upon?*

This question helps you to identify *instances of success* (George et al., 1999), which can help you both to identify solutions to whatever problem prompted the meeting. However, if the parent presents as particularly agitated and you suspect this question would not yield a positive response, you may pursue a second option of simply complimenting the parent. Remember when you asked about those things, the parent appreciates about their student? Well, those attributes didn't come out of nowhere. Be sure to compliment the parent on their contributions toward raising this young human with positive qualities. If you are like most administrators, you may be concerned about the extra time this before-the-conversation conversation may take, but we believe that taking time to set a constructive tone will be worth it. You will appear trustworthy and sincerely interested in doing your best to be helpful.

Ask What the Parent Wants: Finding Their Best Hopes

You have now created a friendly environment, ready to build solutions together, so you really want to learn exactly what they want, and they probably really want to tell you! Solution-focused administrators seek out what parents want by asking a *best hope* question (i.e., *what are your best hopes from our talking?* (Ratner et al., 2012). Here, you should be careful in your wording, as it can make the difference between staying problem-focused and moving into solution-focused conversations. Consider the difference between the following two invitations:

What would you like to discuss today?

What are you hoping will come from our meeting today?

In the first question, the focus is on what will be discussed during the meeting and most individuals will launch into talking about a problem. Quickly, all of your efforts to begin a solution-focused conversation will be for naught. In the second question, asking what "will come from" focuses on what will result from your discussion. Ascertaining what the parent wants/expects you to do is what you really want to know, right? By cutting to the chase in this way, you may recoup some of the time you spent identifying strengths and complimenting.

Compliment the Values Behind the Parent's Complaints

Of course, it is still possible that the parent will prefer to complain, as they may not know what they want to come from the conversation. They just know that something is wrong and want you to know about it. If this happens, look for the values behind their complaints. If the parent talks about their child missing an opportunity that they perceive others are getting, they likely value fairness. If the parent complains about a teacher "not liking" their child, they value relationships and their child feeling accepted at school. And, the fact that they are talking with you at all indicates that they value the role of education in their child's life. When an administrator is faced with a complaining parent, they may begin to feel anxious and defensive. However, when engaging to identify their values, you are less likely to take the feedback personally.

Once you have a couple of values identified, you are now ready to interject with a compliment that validates the parent and their concerns. Following this compliment, *re-ask* the best hopes question like this: *Not every parent would take the time to reach out. It really tells me how much you care about your child's education. What do you want to happen as a result of meeting with me?* By asking this question, the administrator helps to create a useful direction for the conversation and the parent feels heard.

Asking Difference Questions

When parents respond with specific requests for what they want to happen, and their requests may or may not be possible, the solution-focused mindset can assist you in finding alternatives that are possible. For instance:

> *I want my child to be in Mr. C's class.*
>
> *I want my child to have XYZ accommodation.*

Regardless of whether or not you are able to grant their request (but especially in cases when you cannot), consider asking a *difference question* (Ajmal & Ratner, 2020):

What differences in your child's behavior do you anticipate happening if they are in Mr. C's class?

What difference will it make to your child's ability to learn if they are given this accommodation?

Typically, a parent's request is not an outcome they desire; it is what they believe will facilitate what they want to happen. They want their child to be accepted, to have good relationships, to learn well, to be prepared for the future, and to be successful both in school and in life. Also, they want these goals to be met with as little disruption to their family life as possible (e.g., they don't want to spend hours on homework or deal with meltdowns on a regular basis). They may make specific requests because they believe the outcomes they describe to you will be the result. Solution-focused trainer Teri Pichot (personal communication, 2014) once made the analogy of going to Chicago. She may say that she wants a flight to Chicago. In reality, she just wants to get to Chicago, but she could take a plane, bus, or car to get there. There are other methods of transportation. Similarly, there may be other ways to facilitate the parent's goal for their child, especially when it is not possible. By asking difference questions, you can determine the parent's ultimate *preferred future* (Iveson, 1994).

Developing a Preferred Future

Helping someone create a preferred future is a hallmark of the solution-focused approach and comes from Steve de Shazer's (1988) *miracle question*, which asked the client to describe how things would be "if a miracle happened" and the problem was no longer an issue. The previously mentioned parent goal of what a parent wants to happen (e.g., child's success in school and life) is an example of how the best hopes answer can help to describe a preferred future. In most cases, the parent has a goal that you can get on board with. Of course, you want their child to be successful! When listening to the parent's preferred future, it can be easy for administrators to immediately jump into problem-solving. We urge you to resist this inclination! If you give suggestions without truly understanding the parent's preferred future, they will likely be back in your office with new demands before you know it. Be cautious of making assumptions; adopt a curious stance and make sure you understand what they mean to convey in regard to what they want.

Take the preferred future of "success in school" for example. How does the parent define success? Is it a matter of better grades? Is it related to their student learning and being happy in school? Does it mean that the student will be prepared for the next grade level? Does the parent measure success by how much is required of *them* at home? Values come into play when defining success, and the school and the parent(s) may have very different operational definitions. It is very important to understand the parent's idea of success in school.

Exploring specific details of the parent's preferred future will better equip you to collaborate with the parent to find common goals. The more detailed description you can get from a parent regarding their preferred future, the more material with which you have to work with and to suggest that they can help you with. A very important detail to obtain relates to what the parent will notice when their preferred future is starting to materialize, even in the smallest of ways. It may be that there are already small glimmers of this preferred future coming true that they want more of. Perhaps there was a time that their child did get along with a teacher or took a test/assignment where their child performed well. These are successes that can become solutions that you may build upon. Your partnership with the parent becomes much for fun as you both agree to be on the lookout for small instances of success and take time to celebrate those successes. What parent wouldn't want a school administrator who can be a fellow cheerleader for their child? The following case illustrates how these strategies may be used.

Case Scenario

A high school sophomore has been consistently sent to the office for disrespectful and vulgar behavior. As a result, he has been suspended three times during the semester and faces a possible expulsion if the behaviors continue. The parent is angry and demands a meeting with the administrator after talking to the assistant administrator. Observe the sample conversation below:

Administrator: Thanks for coming to talk to me today and taking time out of your day. Tell me, what do you hope comes from our conversation?

Parent: Well, I am sick and tired of the way my son is being treated in this school. He is a good kid and the suspensions he has been given this semester have cost me time at my job, and I need to see those suspensions stop. Apparently, someone just does not like my son. He is really a good kid.

Administrator: Okay. Can you tell me what difference it might make someday when those suspensions stop?

Parent: It would make a big difference. I wouldn't worry about losing my job. I wouldn't worry about leaving him at home all day while I work. I would know he was in school learning something. He is actually the first in our family who may graduate from high school. He can't graduate if he is kicked out all of the time.

Administrator: Okay. I am impressed that you want so much for your son. Tell me, what is it about your son that perhaps we don't recognize yet?

Parent: He is a good kid. He helps his uncle at the car repair shop. He watches his younger siblings when I work late.

I think he is smart too. His uncle said he is good at repairing computer parts of cars.

Administrator: That is good to know! Is he in a computer course here?

Parent: No, he is behind in credits so he is still in basics.

Administrator: Okay. So, if we were to find a way to get your son to stay here in school, and not be suspended anymore, would that help?

Parent: It really would.

Administrator: So, in order to see things in your son like you do, what do you think he might need to start doing more of here at school?

Parent: Well, first, his teachers would have to be nicer. They are so sarcastic to him. He tells me what they say. I'm not surprised he curses at them.

Administrator: Okay. Thanks for that. But I wonder what the teachers might need to see your son do in class, too, so they would back off? You obviously see him do good things at home. By the way, I am fine with talking to his teachers and asking them to start noticing things that your son would be willing to try and show them.

Parent: I guess he would have to straighten up. If he could be like he is at his uncle's car repair shop, they would see a different kid!

Administrator: Sounds good. Is it okay if I go get your son so he can hear your ideas and hopes for him? I want him to know too that his teachers and I would like to see him as you do very soon.

The administrator then may go get the student out of class and ask the student to join the parent and the administrator together. By talking to the student in front of the parent with a solution-focused mindset, wanting to get to know the student differently, the relationship has a better chance of changing between the student and the administrator. It also involves the parent in the conversation so the parent sees that the administrator is truly interested in bringing out the best in the child. That observation by the parent can go a long way to supporting the school and helping to remind the student to show his better side at school.

In this real scenario, the administrator not only brought the student in to talk to the parent and himself but also suggested that the young man connect with the computer science teacher as a possible assistant. The administrator's suggestion came from what the parent said the student was good at. Then, the administrator did more. He literally walked the student down to the computer lab after the meeting that day to suggest to the computer science teacher that the student was interested in computers and wanted to be an assistant in class. The administrator and the student shook hands after meeting the computer science teacher. The administrator then told the student that while there were rules he had to follow to stay in school, he was going to start watching out for the kid his parent told him about that day. The administrator also wrote emails to the student's teachers, asking them to watch out for things that the student began to do better at. He suggested that the teachers call on the student to help with computers or other tasks, to bring out the student's competencies. The student was shocked by the attention he began to get at school, and so was the parent. While it may seem that there were many more steps that the administrator took that day, it paid off in that the student became more engaged in school, and the suspensions ceased.

Solution-Focused Parent Conversations: Step-by-Step

The steps taken in this scenario seem simple, and yet they require a shift in mindset away from prioritizing the rules and punishing the student. If you are having a parent conference, where a student is repeatedly being suspended, the punishments are not working. A wise solution-focused administrator always considers what has been tried and does something different.

Although it is very important to focus on rules, listening to a parent's true desire for their child and then turning the responsibility back on to both the child and the parent has shown to be much more effective. The following steps were taken in the illustrated conversation.

Ask about the Parent's Best Hopes
No matter the complaint of the parent, always listen first and resist asking why a problem is occurring or saying what policies had to be followed. Neither response will go well, especially if the parent is upset. Instead, once the parent seems finished, ask the best hopes question to help focus the conversation on the outcome. Should the outcome, as mentioned earlier, seem a little far-fetched, the simple difference question of *"What difference would that make for you?"* can go a long way to connect with a parent. In this case, the parent's job was in jeopardy. The parent also wanted the son to graduate. These two "wants" of the parent were listened to and led to the parent and son helping the administrator make it happen.

Compliment the Parent on What He/She Wants for the Child
Compliments are unexpected in many parent conversations, especially stressful ones, yet compliments suggest that the school administrator is "not all bad!" Asking a compliment goes a long way to gaining compliance, lessening resistance, and focusing on the outcome, which will involve the parent and the student, as well as staff at school.

Inquire Who the Child Is at Home/Work/Sports
By finding out about different venues where the students show better behaviors, you may discover new strategies for dealing with and reaching the student. For example, when the parent mentioned the student's computer competencies, the administrator then had additional ideas to consider to reach the desired outcome and increase collaboration and cooperation with the

student. Also, learning about such times when better behaviors occur are the "instances of success" mentioned throughout this book. By learning about times when the student behaves and responds better to others and adults and what interests bring out the student's good traits, you can compile a plan. This not only impresses the parent with your sincerity and implementation of the student's positive traits but also lessens resistance from the student! And, here's a bonus—As you show the parent that you are sincerely interested in helping their child, the parent is more likely to support the school. When students see their parents support the school rather than complain about the school, they take notice.

Plan the Next Steps with the Parent and Child in the Same Room

By bringing everyone together, the parent and student get to see another side of you too, and that encourages the parent to align with you. This alignment with the parent, once experienced by the student, lessens a "triangle" where all three persons are out of alignment with each other, making the school seem to be the culprit of the problem. By including the student in the conversation at this point, you can go over expectations of the school and step into solution building, so the student can see your desire to help. It is important to again mention the power of going one step further to help create opportunities for students to show their competencies, such as visiting with the computer teacher in the case.

This part of the conversation also leads to asking the student, *"what might your teachers need to see you do for the next few days, to show them the child that your parent knows?"* If the student seems taken aback by this question (and many are), wait for answers. While the student thinks, ask the parent the same question and let the parent expand on "what else" the student could begin to show the teachers. This part of the conversation can be truly priceless, as you listen to solution building happening. If the parent suggests that teachers be nicer again, agree that such a request is reasonable and that you intend to ask the teachers to watch out for the student the parent knows so nicer reactions happen.

Act on the Plan
End the conversation by suggesting a plan based on instances of success from the conversation with everyone present. Talk to the student about the plan and follow through immediately, contacting teachers, coaches, or other staff who need to know the plan. Write an email with the student and parent still in the office to each teacher, asking them to watch out for new behaviors that the student will try out. Doing this is absolutely essential, as it will hopefully change the way that the teachers see the student. Doing it before the conversation ends also keeps you efficient.

Follow Up
It may seem like one too many steps to take, but following up the next day conveys to the student that you are watching and seeing that he/she is following through too. When you do this, let the student know that you will also check with the teachers too, to find out *what is going better.* Continue to do email check-ins with the teachers so the student knows that the staff is watching for better behaviors too.

Solution-Focused Parent Conference (Reproducible)

1. **Ask about the best hopes question.**
   So, what are your best hopes for our time today?
   What difference would that make to you or your child?
2. **Compliment the parent on what he/she wants for their child.**
   I appreciate your desire to make things better for your child. You took time to come here today and that tells me how important your child is to you. I am interested in helping you achieve some things that are important to you.
3. **Inquire about who the child is at home/work/sports that the parent is proud of.**
   Before we go on, tell me more about your child and things about him/her that I can learn about. What is he/she good at, interested in outside of school, etc.?
4. **Plan the next steps with the student and parent together.**
   Thanks, _____ (student) for joining us. Your parent wants the following things to start happening for you. (Repeat parent's best hopes.) I would like for you to tell me what you might be willing to try out so we can achieve what your parent wants.
5. **Act on the plan with parent and student in the room. Send an email:**

   Dear Teachers,
   I am working with _____ and his/her parent. Together, we have come up with a plan so the student becomes more successful in your classes. Over the next few days, I will share a plan with you. Once you receive the plan, please watch for changes that the student tries to make in your classroom to show he/she is trying to improve. Your observations will be helpful to me as I keep in touch with you, the student, and the parent.

6. **Follow up with the student and teachers consistently for a short time.**

   Check in with the student and teacher(s) the next day and for a short time to ensure that changes are taking place. Ask: "What's going better?" This will encourage people to seek what is successful rather than what is not successful.

Sentence Stems for Parent Conversations (Reproducible)

- *I want to thank you for taking time out of your day to talk with me. It really tells me how much you care about your child's education.* (Compliment)
- *Before we get started, I want to ask—what is going well right now for your child at school that we want to make sure we don't mess up?* (Focus on strengths)
- *How can I be helpful to you? What needs to come out of this conversation today so that you can say this is helpful?* (Best hopes)
- *What difference will that make for you? For your child?* (Difference question)
- Check your understanding and validate their concerns.
- *Are there some days that are better than others? What is happening when it is better?* (Exception-seeking)
- *What will you notice when things are starting to turn around? What might tell you that things are getting a bit better?* (Noticing instances of success)
- *What will you have done to facilitate that happening, and what might the school have done?* (Solution-building)
- Request that they pay attention to times that things are going better, even a little bit, and to let you know (via email). (Noticing task)

Chapter Tips for Administrators

1. Consider putting assumptions about the parent or student aside.
2. Never give up on a student.
3. Seek out other aspects/talents of a student and get to know who else the student is. What are their interests and assets?

4. Seek instances of success, times when the student is not in trouble or is more successful.
5. Always let the student co-create the preferred future with you and the parent.
6. Mention to the student and parent the importance of taking small steps, one day at a time.
7. See yourself as a co-collaborator with a student and parent, which will make it easier to uphold policy.
8. Always involve the teacher(s) who are involved with the concern of the student and inform them that the student wants to make changes. Ask them to watch for change. This will help the teacher also see the student differently and react differently.

References

Ajmal, Y., & Ratner, H. (2020). *Solution focused practice in schools: 80 ideas and strategies*. Routledge.

De Shazer, S. (1988). *Clues: Investigating solutions in brief therapy*. W. W. Norton.

Franklin, C., Streeter, C. L., Webb, L., & Guz, S. (2018). *Solution focused brief therapy in alternative schools: Ensuring student success and preventing dropouts*. Routledge.

George, E., Iveson, C., & Ratner, H. (1999). *Problem to solution: Brief therapy with individuals and families* (Revised and expanded edition). Brief Therapy Press.

Iveson, C. (1994). *Preferred futures, exceptional pasts* [Conference presentation]. European Brief Therapy Association Conference, Stockholm, Sweden.

Ratner, H., George, E., & Iveson, C. (2012). *Solution focused brief therapy: 100 key points and techniques*. Routledge.

4

Solution-Focused Teacher Supervision

Marcella D. Stark

In one private university, faculty in a college of education are called upon to provide peer teaching observations to help one another improve their teaching. A counselor educator observed their educational leadership colleague lecture on developmental instructional supervision in an instructional supervision course. In their description of developmental instructional supervision, Glickman et al. (2014) pose that administrators consider the teacher's level of expertise and match their supervision approach accordingly on a continuum of directive control with the supervisor taking responsibility (e.g., *I want you to include a pair-and-share activity in your lesson*) to nondirective promoting teacher responsibility (e.g., *what ideas do you have for keeping students engaged?*). The goal of this model is to move toward a nondirective stance in which teachers are empowered to take responsibility for their own improvement. When uncertain about the teacher's developmental level, Glickman et al. (2014) advise supervisors to begin in a place of collaboration, a midline approach on this continuum that encourages shared problem-solving and decision-making. The aspiring school administrators in this graduate class struggled with this concept, because they felt their strengths were in being decisive problem-solvers. After all, aren't educational leaders put in charge to make decisions? Coming from a counseling background, I raised my hand and shared a few ideas of how they might use a collaborative approach, and the idea for this book was born.

Like the students in the class, you may believe that it is your responsibility to come up with solutions to problems, especially with less-experienced teachers. Isn't that what *solution-focused* means? If you've read the initial chapters of this book, you know that the answer is "no", but let's first begin with a discussion of what supervision means.

Instructional Supervision v. Teacher Evaluation

A distinction must be made between instructional supervision and teacher evaluation. Glickman et al. (2014) described supervision as promoting teacher growth through a process of formative feedback that is uniquely tailored to meet the teacher's developmental needs. Evaluation involves summative feedback on job performance that also informs an administrator's decision making related to teachers' professional development, salaries, and contract renewals.

Hazi (2018) noted that teacher observations have long been used as a form of evaluation to make personnel decisions. She suggested evaluation and supervision are "similar, yet not identical" (p. 186). Hazi described the evaluation process as an administrator visiting a classroom to observe and complete ratings using a formal instrument and later meeting with the teacher to share the ratings. This process only partially follows the structure of the clinical supervision cycle (Cogan, 1973):

1. establishing the teacher-supervisor relationship,
2. planning with the teacher,

3. planning the strategy of observation,
4. observing instruction,
5. analyzing the teaching-learning process,
6. planning the strategy of the conference,
7. the conference, and
8. renewed planning.

As the graduate students learned about this process and combined it with a solution-focused approach, they commented how they wished they had been supervised in such a manner. Some reported that, as teachers, their own administrators simply performed a walk-through observation and left the completed checklist in their box, providing them with no supervision at all. Their experiences were in keeping with Hazi's claim that most administrators do not have time to engage in thoughtful conversations during post-observation meetings.

For some school districts, the answer for supervision lies in employing instructional coaches or promoting a peer coaching model for supervision. However, as budgets shrink and teacher workloads increase, this is not always a viable option. The reality is that most administrators will have dual roles of evaluator and supervisor. Mette et al. (2017) acknowledged the intersection of evaluation and the time-intensive process of supervision, and they suggested that the combination has the potential to create a better-functioning school. They noted a helpful overlap between the two functions of supporting and monitoring teachers in targeted areas of improvement and developing a collaborative culture that values teacher feedback. The principals in their study focused on the strengths of teachers. These concepts are in line with Stark et al.'s (2017) article on how administrators tasked with the dual roles of supervisor and evaluator may use a solution-focused approach, which focuses on strengths, to promote teacher development.

Solution-Focused Supervision

Solution-focused supervision is an adaptation of solution-focused brief therapy (SFBT; de Shazer et al., 1986), which began as an approach to family therapy and has since been shown to be effective for a variety of issues in school settings (Kim et al., 2017). The solution-focused supervisor will use the same principles when working with supervisees (e.g., teachers). A common misunderstanding of the solution-focused approach is that it is about solving problems, but in one of his early books, Steve de Shazer (1988) suggested that it is more important to focus on what is working than waste time dissecting a problem. de Shazer would later become "known for reversing the ... interview process by asking clients to describe a detailed solution of the problem ..., thereby shifting the focus of treatment from problems to solutions" (Trepper et al., 2006, p. 133). This concept is counterintuitive to many administrators who have been trained to ask "why". Although "knowing your why" can be a helpful motivation strategy, attempting to know the root of a problem can result in a time-consuming process that often leads to everyone involved feeling overwhelmed and defeated.

Solution-Focused Mindset

Curious/Not Knowing

The solution-focused approach is a mindset (with accompanying helpful strategies) that is *not knowing* (Anderson & Goolishian, 1992), strengths-based, and collaborative. With a not-knowing mindset, we are curious about another person's experience while reserving judgment about the problem, asking what caused it, and any potential solutions. In the context of teacher supervision, we trust the expertise of the teacher (yes, even new teachers are the experts in what happens in their classrooms) and attempt to understand their experience. As we ask questions to learn about their perspectives, we look for strengths that might be amplified. Every teacher is doing something that is working, and likely, many things. In solution-focused teacher supervision, the teacher learns to recognize and do more of what works. Rather than the administrator declaring the teacher's strengths and areas for growth, a collaborative conversation takes place in which the teacher is empowered to recognize those areas and set goals for growing their craft. Thomas (1994) referred to solution-focused supervision as the "coaxing of expertise" (p. 11).

Collaborative

This collaborative stance may be challenging for some administrators. In my work with administrators, I noted that while they strived to build a collaborative community of educators, some had difficulty trusting the expertise of some teachers, especially less-experienced teachers. Thomas (2010, 2013) makes analogies to semaphore, metaphor, and 2x4 when when giving feedback to supervisees. Although he was referencing clinical supervisors working with counselor trainees, the same principles apply to administrators providing instructional supervision to teachers. *Semaphore* refers to a messaging system with the use of flags. In this analogy, the administrator points the teacher in a direction, but it is up to the teacher whether or not they choose to act upon this direction. Using *metaphor*, the administrator may share a story about what another teacher did (e.g., using experiential exercises in teaching, managing classroom behavior). Again, the teacher is left to see how the metaphor relates to their own situation and what strategies they may implement in their own teaching. Conversely, Thomas jokingly references the *2x4 piece of lumber* to knock the supervisee over the head with an unequivocal directive that must be followed. There is no question that administrators hold ultimate responsibility for what takes place on their campuses, and there are times that the administrator must distinctly communicate decisions without consideration of teacher perspectives. For instance, if a kindergarten teacher wants to build a bonfire in their classroom, of course, the administrator must be clear in telling the teacher that she cannot do so. However, some administrators may use this as their go-to stance. Although it may be easier to simply tell teachers what they should do, such authoritarian practices do not empower teachers to take responsibility for making good decisions on their own.

One new administrator commented that as much as he tried to use a solution-focused approach to supervision, his teachers refused to work in a collaborative manner. They had acclimated to the authoritarian culture developed by previous administrators, and they did not trust that he was actually interested in their perspectives or that he wouldn't use any statements against them. Of course, trust takes time to develop, but administrators should not pretend that they don't hold power over teachers. Thomas (2013) suggested that the power differential should be acknowledged, but that supervisors should "work to flatten hierarchy and build collaboration" (p. 48). Administrators may follow this suggestion by being transparent in explaining the supervision and evaluation processes, being clear about where teachers have a say (e.g., setting professional development goals) and where they do not (scores on evaluation rubric). Returning to that graduate class of aspiring administrators who struggled with the "how" of collaboration, all of the strategies discussed in Chapter 1 of this book may be applied to teacher supervision.

Solution-Focused Strategies

Complimenting

Complimenting is the strategy that appears to come most naturally to administrators. It is not unique to the solution-focused approach, and in recent years with such a high rate of resignations occurring among educators, administrators are especially aware of their faculty's vulnerability and the need for compliments. Administrators tread carefully when supervising and evaluating their teachers. In the solution-focused approach, complimenting is used to draw attention to instances of success. More than a mere gesture of appreciation, the administrator will be specific in their compliments and ask "how" questions to draw out the teacher's tactics that resulted in success. Nims (2007) referred to this as the "wow and how" strategy (p. 57): *Wow, your entire class is on task! How did you get them to behave so well?*

Future-Focused Questions

A trademark of the solution-focused approach is "the miracle question" (de Shazer et al., 2021, p. 37): *Suppose you went to bed tonight and a miracle happened while you were sleeping. Tomorrow morning when you come to school, your class is engaged and you are the best educator you could be. What is the first thing you would notice that tells you this miracle has happened?* Using vernacular more common in education settings, an administrator may ask: *When I do my next walk-through, what might I see that shows positive changes in the area we've been discussing?* Future-focused questions like this help teachers consider what they want to happen in the future. As they describe their preferred future in detail, the administrator helps them to identify small, concrete changes they might make to make that preferred future a reality.

Scaling

Once a description of the teacher's preferred future (explained in Chapter 1) is provided, an administrator may ask a teacher to use a scale (e.g., 0–10, 1–5) to indicate how close they are to their preferred future. Follow-up questions may be asked to determine how they got to that number (assuming that they used to be lower on the scale), revealing successful strategies previously used, as well as describe what the next higher number might look like. When supervision is a separate process, the scale can be truly teacher-driven. However, when using an established rubric for evaluation, it is essential to be transparent about the process. Teachers will feel betrayed if collaboration is only a false pretense as if you've pulled the rug out from under them with a bad evaluation. However, the strategy of scaling may still be useful. Discuss with the teacher what each score on the rubric might look like in their classroom, strategies they've used thus far to reach an identified level on the rubric, and small steps that might demonstrate the next higher level.

Using Tentative Language

If you deem it necessary to provide suggestions, Insoo Kim Berg suggested *hedging* or the use of tentative language (Rudes et al., 1997; Thomas, 2013) in supervision. You might consider Thomas's (2010, 2013) analogy of semaphore, where the teacher is free to disagree. See what I did there? By using tentative language such as *You might consider* or *I wonder if ...*, you communicate that the teacher may take your advice or go in a different direction. At the end of the day, the teacher is responsible for their own classroom and must adapt strategies to their own unique style and their own classes. Instead of outright telling the teacher what to do, by asking the teacher to consider a given option, the administrator gives credit to the teacher if they decide to follow through with the suggestion.

Asking for Feedback

At the end of a conference with a teacher, you may again foster a spirit of collaboration by asking for feedback. It should be clear to both of you how the meeting went and if the teacher has well-defined ideas about what they will do moving forward. Whereas you may believe the meeting went great, the teacher may have a different perspective. Remember that it is currently a difficult era for teachers, and regardless of the evaluation scores, you want them to feel respected and affirmed. You won't get feedback unless you ask.

Research Findings

Whereas most of the research conducted on the solution-focused approach in schools has focused on student and teacher outcomes, I have embarked on researching the concepts outlined in this chapter with aspiring administrators (i.e., graduate students) in a clinical supervision cycle (McGhee & Stark, 2018, 2021) and with administrators more broadly (not yet published). The aspiring administrators shared that solution-focused language helped them to promote teacher reflection and empower teachers to assume more responsibility for decision making in their classrooms. The aspiring administrators also credited the approach with giving them more confidence in their leadership abilities and took comfort that they didn't have to know all the answers to be helpful. My more recent research with participants who are already working as administrators also showed that they had a positive view of the approach, and they successfully used the strategies described in this chapter across many activities (e.g., student discipline, parent meetings, trainings) including teacher supervision and evaluation. The practices I observed are portrayed in the following case scenario.

Case Scenario: Pre- and Post-Observation Conferences

An assistant principal is charged with conducting an evaluation for a special education (SPED) teacher using an instrument required by her school district. She has more than 10 years of teaching experience, but she is fairly new to the administrator role. Based on her belief that teachers are experts, she used a solution-focused approach. In the following case scenario, you will see a condensed version of both a pre-observation conference and a post-observation conference. Note the strategies used in each.

Pre-Observation Conference

AP: Good morning. I'm excited to visit your class! I had a different specialty when I taught and I look forward to learning from you. (curious, not knowing stance; valued teacher's expertise)

Teacher: Well, you're welcome to visit my class anytime.

AP: Thank you. I appreciate that. While there will be an official "observation" as part of the evaluation, I'll be doing a few informal walk-throughs. If there is something in particular you'd like me to see, just let me know. (invited collaboration)

Teacher: Sure thing.

AP: What do you think is especially important for me to know about your class? (invited collaboration)

Teacher: Well, I have multiple ages in this class. The fifth graders help out the younger ones.

AP: That's so nice! I love the culture you've created in your classroom. How did you do that? (specific compliment followed by "how" question to draw out details of teacher's strengths)

Teacher: A couple of them have been in this class for more than one year, so I try to change things up. For instance, this year I'm using popsicle sticks to assign roles.

AP: That's really creative. Well, I don't want to take up too much of your time. I brought a copy of the rubric that I'll be using. It was based on general education, but I encourage you to make it your own. [proceeds to review the rubric, pointing out adaptation for SPED setting] Which area of "refinement" would you like to focus on? (minimized hierarchy through transparency, empowered teacher)

Teacher: I like this rubric. I think I'd like to focus on communication. I'm pretty confident with my students, but I want to communicate better with their parents.

AP: That's a great goal. It's so important to develop good relationships with parents. Where might you put yourself on a scale of 1–5 with this goal? What have you done so far to reach this number? (affirmed teacher's ideas, scaling)

Teacher: Probably a three and a half. I send notes home letting them know something their child did well.

AP: What would tell you that you're at a four? (future-focused question)

Teacher: Hmm. I'd probably give the parents more compliments when we interact.

AP: That's a wonderful idea. Please try that and let me know how it goes. [Returning to the rubric] Talk to me a little about the overarching objective for the lesson I'll be observing. How will I know when I see … [quoted language from rubric]? (brought teacher back to the rubric and asked future-focused question)

Teacher: Teacher shared the "see, touch, say" strategy for literacy and reviewed the class morning routine.

AP: Nice! It sounds like the read aloud gives you flexibility, and it relates to one of the essential skills mentioned in the rubric. I'll be coming at 10 am on Wednesday, and it would be great if I could see an artifact that demonstrates what we discussed. When we meet after the observation, we can talk more about this communication piece. Until then, I encourage you to think about action steps and let me know if there is anything else you want to focus on (amplified success by pointing out how what the teacher is already doing relates to essential skills, provided suggestions to help the teacher be successful but ended by returning power to the teacher). [Following the observation, this assistant principal sent an email to the teacher to give compliments and validate strengths she noticed that may not be addressed in the evaluation rubric]:

Teacher X. I so enjoyed visiting your class today! I loved the small group activity you facilitated and the respectful way you managed the student who kept interrupting you. I look forward to our post-observation conference next week.

Post-Observation Conference

AP: Good afternoon. I appreciated the opportunity to watch you in action the other day! I'm still learning, and I want you to know that I truly see you as the expert in teaching in a contained classroom. I want to hear your perceptions, but I also want to respect your time. (valued teacher's expertise, curious stance)

AP and the teacher then look over the dimensions on the rubric, with the AP sharing anchors for each score on the rubric (distinguished through improvement). (provided transparency about the evaluation process)

AP: I'm curious to hear your perceptions. On a scale of 1–5, how close did you come to reaching the goals you had set? (scaling)

Teacher: I'd say about a four. [She then went on to explain the crafts she had planned].

AP: These are some great ideas. Keep in mind that this rubric is completed at a certain point in time. I can only evaluate what I see. Using the same scale based on the limitation of what I observed, how might you rate yourself on each of these domains? (gives reminder of evaluation limitations but quickly returns to teacher's perceptions)

[Teacher responds, going through each of the domains.]

Teacher: For my students, I have to focus more on what is in their IEP. Also, Sally was having a bad day when you came.

AP: Hey, I get it. There's a difference between plans for the whole class and an individual student's IEP. And sometimes their personal plans are more important than the academic goal for the class. And don't worry about a bad day. Bad days are when I really get to see your craft! (affirms teacher's perspective)

[AP asked more questions about SPED content before sharing her own ratings (~20 minutes into the meeting)]. (invites collaboration by asking for teacher's self-ratings first)

AP: I especially liked how well you scaffolded the content when you asked ... [pointed out intentional questions that the teacher had asked] and how you made each child feel successful. You know, I'm wondering how these communication skills might relate to your interactions with parents. (amplifying strength by connecting it to the teacher's own targeted area for growth)

Teacher: Hmm. I'll have to think about that.

[AP reviewed areas of refinement and reinforcement, but ended with a summary of the teacher's strengths.] (compliments)

AP: If you have any questions or thoughts about this process, I'd love your feedback. Thank you for meeting with me. I appreciate your time. (invited feedback)

In this scenario, the assistant principal had a job to do. Although the teacher (and her students) had different self-initiated goals, she had to conduct the evaluation using a specific rubric that required artifacts (observation of specific teaching strategies). Throughout both meetings, she affirmed the teacher's perspectives, communicated that she valued her expertise, and sought collaboration. She sought collaboration by being transparent about the rubric and the evaluation process, and she called attention to the teacher's strengths and gave specific feedback when needed to help the teacher be successful.

So how might these concepts be useful to you the next time you conduct a teacher evaluation? You'll have to try them to find out. Consider copying the sentence stems on the following page and look them over just before you begin your next pre-observation conference. And if you have a minute, send me an email. I'd love to hear how it goes.

Sentence Stems for Supervision and Evaluation Meetings (Reproducible)

- *Part of my role as administrator is to evaluate you using this tool. I trust that you have some ideas about your own strengths and areas for growth. Let's review this tool together. Which areas would you like us to focus on in this meeting?* (flattening hierarchy with transparency)
- *When is a time that every student was engaged, even for a portion of the class?* (identifying instances of success)
- *Wow! How were you able to make that happen?* (gathering details of strengths/past success)
- *On a scale from 1 to 10, with 1 indicating not very successful and 10 indicating your ideal, how would you rate your achievement of the goal we've discussed? (or your overall teaching of the class observed?) What do you think attributed to you to reaching that level? If you were a half-rating higher, what would have changed?* (scaling)
- *In relation to our earlier scale, where do you hope to be by X? What will you have done to make that happen? What will tell you that it was a good move?* (setting goals)
- *I have this idea that I'm going to throw out for you to consider. I wonder ...* (tentative language)
- *How was this meeting for you? What was helpful about our meeting?* (seeking feedback)

Chapter Tips for Administrators

- Acknowledge the expertise of your teachers.
- Adopt a curious stance and allow them to teach you about their subject matter and classrooms.
- Affirm their perspectives and validate their concerns and challenges.
- Look for what your teachers are doing well.

- Give specific compliments and ask "how" questions to gather details about their instances of success.
- Ask future-focused questions to learn about teacher's preferred future (for their class, for their professional growth, etc.).
- Ask scaling questions to encourage reflectiveness and assist goal setting.
- Use tentative language to encourage collaboration and empower teachers to make their own decisions.
- Be transparent about the evaluation process. Share the rubric and discuss the specific indicators for each rating. When applicable, discuss any idiosyncrasies related to their unique class setting.
- Ask for feedback about the supervision/evaluation process.

References

Anderson, H., & Goolishian, H. (1992). The client is the expert: A not-knowing approach to therapy. In S. McNamee & K. J. Gergen (Eds.), *Therapy as social construction* (pp. 2–39). Sage.

Cogan, M. (1973). *Clinical supervision*. Houghton Mifflin Company.

de Shazer, S. (1988). *Clues: Investigating solutions in brief therapy*. W. W. Norton & Co.

de Shazer, S., Berg, I. K., Lipchik, E., Nunnally, E., Molnar, A., Gingerich, W., & Weiner-Davis, M. (1986). Brief therapy: Focused solution development. *Family Process, 25*(2), 207–221. https://doi.org/10.1111/j.1545-5300.1986.00207.x

de Shazer, S., Dolan, Y., Korman, H., Trepper, T., McCollum, E., & Berg, I. K. (2021). *More than miracles: The state of the art of solution-focused brief therapy*. Routledge.

Glickman, C. D., Gordon, S. P., & Ross-Gordon, J. M. (2014). *SuperVision and instructional leadership: A developmental approach* (9th ed.). Pearson.

Hazi, H. M. (2018). Coming to understand the wicked problem of teacher evaluation. In S. J. Zepeda & J. A. Ponticell (Eds.), *The Wiley handbook of educational supervision* (pp. 183–207). John Wiley & Sons. https://doi.org/10.1002/9781119128304.ch8

Kim, J., Kelly, M., & Franklin, C. (2017). *Solution-focused brief therapy in schools: A 360-degree view of the research and practice principles*. Oxford University Press.

McGhee, M. W., & Stark, M. D. (2018). Promoting collegial teacher supervision: Applying solution-focused strategies in a clinical supervision cycle. *International Journal of Leadership in Education*, *21*(6), 726–740. https://doi.org/10.1080/13603124.2018.1463458

McGhee, M. W., & Stark, M. D. (2021). Empowering teachers through instructional supervision: Using solution focused strategies in a leadership preparation program. *Journal of Educational Supervision*, *4*(1), 41–65. https://doi.org/10.31045/jes.4.1.5

Mette, I. M., Range, B. G., Anderson, J., Hvidston, D. J., Nieuwenhuizen, L., & Doty, J. (2017). The wicked problem of the intersection between supervision and evaluation. *International Electronic Journal of Elementary Education*, *9*(3), 709–724.

Nims, D. R. (2007). Integrating play therapy techniques into solution-focused brief therapy. *International Journal of Play Therapy*, *16*, 54–68. https://doi.org/10.1037/1555-6824.16.1.54

Rudes, J., Shilts, L., & Berg, I. K. (1997). Focused supervision seen through a recursive frame analysis. *Journal of Marital and Family Therapy*, *23*(2), 203–215.

Stark, M. D., McGhee, M., & Jimerson, J. B. (2017). Reclaiming instructional supervision: Using solution-focused strategies to promote teacher development. *Journal of Research on Leadership Education*, *12*(3), 215–238. https://doi.org/10.1177/1942775116684895

Thomas, F. N. (1994). Solution-oriented supervision: The coaxing of expertise. *The Family Journal*, *2*(1), 11–17. https://doi.org/10.1177/1066480794021003

Thomas, F. N. (2010). Semaphore, metaphor, two-by-four. In T. S. Nelson (Ed.), *Doing something different: Solution-focused brief therapy practices* (pp. 219–224). Routledge.

Thomas, F. N. (2013). *Solution-focused supervision: A resource-oriented approach to developing clinical expertise*. Springer.

Trepper, T. S., Dolan, Y., McCollum, E. E., & Nelson, T. (2006). Steve de Shazer and the future of solution-focused therapy. *Journal of Marital and Family Therapy*, *32*(2), 133–139. https://doi.org/10.1111/j.1752-0606.2006.tb01595.x

5

A Solution-Focused Approach to Trauma-Informed Practices

Denise J. Krause and Samantha P. Koury

In today's educational landscape, the prevalence of adversity and trauma presents a significant challenge for school administrators. Trauma-informed approaches prioritize understanding, empathy, and resilience to create safe and supportive learning environments for all students and staff. Solution-focused language offers a powerful tool for administrators to adopt trauma-informed practices and support the well-being of students, personnel, and the larger school community. This chapter explores the intersection of solution-focused language and trauma-informed practices in schools and provides practical strategies for you to integrate into your leadership practices.

Trauma and Adversity in Schools

Trauma refers to a psychological injury that results from an event, multiple events, or circumstances that an individual experiences as harmful or life-threatening, and that overwhelms their ability to cope (Substance Abuse and Mental Health Services Administration [SAMHSA], 2023). As a result, traumatic experiences are

TABLE 5.1

Examples of Trauma and Adversity

INDIVIDUAL	COMMUNITY	SCHOOL BASED
Childhood abuse or neglect	Community violence	School shootings
Domestic violence	Hate crimes	Bullying
Single parent household	Poverty	Microaggressions
Death of a loved one	Racism, discrimination	Physical altercations

associated with lasting adverse effects on an individual's functioning and across various domains of well-being. Trauma can be experienced individually (affecting one person) or collectively (e.g., multiple people in a family, group, community, organization/system, etc.). While adversity is not always experienced as trauma, adverse childhood experiences (ACEs) and adverse community environments can also have long-term impacts on individuals across the lifespan—particularly when repeated and prolonged adversities become toxic stress (Ellis & Dietz, 2017; Lê-Cherban et al., 2018; MacLochlainn et al., 2022). Students, parents/caretakers, teachers, staff, and administrators are likely to have histories and/or current experiences of adversity and trauma outside of school that influence their experiences while in school (Garcia et al., 2023; Herrenkohl et al., 2019). They also may experience school-based trauma, where the event or circumstance experienced occurs within the school community (Duane, 2023). Table 5.1 provides a non-exhaustive list for administrators of trauma and adversities that could be experienced by any individual within the school system.

Impact of Trauma and Adversity

The impacts of trauma and adversity are individualized and can be behavioral, emotional, biological, developmental, cognitive, interpersonal, and/or spiritual (SAMHSA, 2023). School district

TABLE 5.2

Example Indicators of Trauma and Adversity in Schools

STUDENTS	PARENTS/ CARETAKERS	SCHOOL PERSONNEL
• Low academic achievement • Poor test scores • Increased absenteeism • Low attention • Dropping out of school • Impulsive behavior • Stomachaches, headaches • Difficulties with peers • Anxiety, depression	• Distrust in school personnel • Disengagement with school and/or child • Substance use • Anxiety/worry for child • Difficulty regulating emotions (i.e., angry outbursts)	• Inconsistent performance • Anxiety, overwhelm • Withdrawal from peers • Increased cynicism, hopelessness • Reduced capacity for empathy, decision-making, and memory • Fatigue, chronic pain

Informed by Davis et al. (2022), MacLochlainn et al. (2022), NCTSN (2008), and SAMHSA (2023).

goals for academic achievement, attendance, test scores, effective teaching, and overall productivity are also directly impacted when students, parents/caretakers, and staff have histories of trauma (National Child Traumatic Stress Network [NCTSN], 2022). Further, school personnel can also be vicariously impacted by working with students and families who have experienced trauma (Sprang & Garcia, 2022). Table 5.2 provides examples of how the impacts of trauma and adversity may show up in your school setting for students, parents/caretakers, and school personnel.

Equally important to note is that adverse life events can also kindle personal growth, at least the subjective experience of it (Tedeschi et al., 2018). Bonanno et al. (2005) state that resilience is often the most commonly observed outcome following a traumatic event. Resilience is the ability to bounce back from adversity, trauma, or significant stress and is more likely to occur in the context of supportive and strong relationships. Resilient individuals can cope with life's challenges and setbacks more effectively, maintain a sense of positivity and optimism, and continue to function effectively despite difficult circumstances. As a vehicle for focusing on what is working and how individuals are managing, solution-focused language builds on coping and competency, even in difficult situations. For you, both promoting resilience and witnessing resilience have a powerful impact that reverberates throughout your school community.

Understanding the Survival Response and Emotion Regulation

One key factor contributing to the manifestation of trauma and adversity indicators in schools is the profound influence of trauma and prolonged adversity on the brain and body, particularly regarding the activation of the survival response system. In the short term, the survival response is designed to ensure our safety by temporarily shutting down the higher areas of the brain (such as the prefrontal cortex) and putting the areas of the brain responsible for our fight, flight, and freeze responses in charge (namely, the amygdala and brain stem) so that we can react to the danger/threat and get to safety (Downey & Greco, 2023; Perry & Winfrey, 2021). However, the survival response system is not meant to be chronically activated. When individuals experience prolonged trauma or adversity, the system becomes sensitized and overactive, resulting in difficulties maintaining a state of emotion regulation and long-term health damaging impacts (Siegel, 2010; van der Kolk, 2015). In the moments when individuals are emotionally dysregulated, it becomes biologically challenging to access the higher parts of the brain responsible for executive functioning, memory, impulse control, empathy, and language (Downey & Greco, 2023; Perry & Winfrey, 2021). Instead of the ability to make conscious and logical decisions, the brain is positioned to react in the face of even minor stressors or neutral stimuli by fighting, fleeing, or shutting down.

You may have had the experience of asking a simple question to a student such as "where are you supposed to be right now?" and they react in an exaggerated way by lashing out or shutting down. While your question is seemingly innocuous, and you might even have thought you were being helpful, the student who has faced chronic stress and/or adversity may experience your question as a threat, thus activating their survival responses. Utilizing solution-focused processes to aid in emotional regulation when the survival response is activated involves amplifying coping mechanisms, strengths, and resources that individuals possess to manage in the here and now (Kim et al., 2017). By guiding individuals to explore past instances of success and envisioning future scenarios where they can apply similar strategies, solution-focused techniques foster a sense of agency and self-efficacy. Through collaborative discussions, you can assist individuals in identifying concrete steps they can take to regulate their emotions in challenging situations, empowering them to cultivate resilience and adaptability.

By shifting the focus from dwelling on negative emotions to envisioning positive outcomes, solution-focused processes encourage individuals to reframe their perspectives and adopt proactive approaches to managing their emotional responses. Work by Byrd-Craven et al. (2008) links the encouragement of continuous "problem talk" and negative emotions to a rise in the stress hormone, cortisol. Over time, increased cortisol levels predict increased anxiety and depression. A solution-focused approach promotes a sense of control and mastery over one's emotions, facilitating emotional regulation and enhancing overall well-being. For instance, have you ever found yourself feeling tired and down after a meeting where teachers spend most of the time complaining? The contagious impact of negativity likely creeps up on you, and you begin to feel helpless and frustrated too. When you are anchored in a more solution-focused stance, you can begin to refocus complaints to possibilities and consequently create more optimism and energy in the room.

A common scenario that can be frustrating for administrators is student absenteeism. When you approach the student from a stance of concern and respect, you are more likely to invite a genuine conversation. Focusing on how the student has managed to come to school on the days that they do attend and what is different about those days will lead to a dialogue about what is possible. Further, your own sense of hopefulness will increase as you invite the student to consider what, in fact, has worked. Conversations aimed at building on previous successes are inherently helpful in creating future successes.

Re-Traumatization

When students, parents/caretakers, and school personnel have experienced trauma or toxic stress, their amygdala is more likely to detect threats even when there is none (van der Kolk, 2015). As a result, you need to be aware that even standard school practices and interactions can inadvertently trigger the survival response. Re-traumatization refers to any procedure, environment, interaction, or situation that replicates someone's history of trauma literally or thematically, putting the individual in a fight and flight or freeze state (Jennings, 2009; Koury et al., 2022). While usually unintentional, re-traumatization is always emotionally harmful and makes it much more difficult for individuals to be successful in school settings academically, professionally, and interpersonally due to the higher parts of the brain being offline.

Of course, you cannot and do not need to be aware of every trauma story within your school. Yet there are trauma themes or dynamics that are common in school settings that are likely to trigger or re-traumatize students, parents/caretakers, and/or school personnel. Table 5.3 provides a few examples of how re-traumatization can occur in schools and solution-focused alternatives. While you are not in the role to treat the trauma of students, parents/caretakers,

TABLE 5.3

Examples of Possible Re-Traumatization in Schools and Solution-Focused Alternatives

SCHOOL PRACTICE OR SITUATION	RE-TRAUMATIZATION THEME	RELATED TRAUMA EXPERIENCE	SOLUTION-FOCUSED RESPONSE
Student asked to re-tell their side of an incident multiple times to different personnel	Being unseen/unheard	Not being believed by adults when a student tried to tell them "their side" *I don't matter*	Begin with *I know you have already told others about what happened. What do you think is important for me to know now?*
Safety drills	Unexpected loud noises	Community violence *I'm not safe*	Alerting pupils and personnel first. Practice what will happen
Faculty meetings focus solely on tasks, information giving, and next steps	Non-acknowledgement of work-related stress	Emotional neglect—psychological needs not met *What's the point in trying?*	Check-ins Acknowledge stress first. Ask about coping. *How are you managing with everything that is going on?*
Parent/caretaker attends a meeting at the school where they notice there is no representation of their culture in signage/décor	Non-inclusive language and messaging	Discrimination, racism *I don't belong here*	Focus on inclusivity and accessibility. Representations of diversity in language, celebrations, and transparent conversations.

and staff, you are positioned to intentionally respond in ways that at least do not cause additional harm and promote resilience. You can create interactions and practices that are both solution-focused and trauma-informed to reduce the likelihood of unintentional re-traumatization of those within the school community.

Trauma-Informed Practices Using the Solution-Focused Approach

A trauma-informed school requires administrators, teachers, and staff to realize the high prevalence of trauma within the school community, recognize the signs of trauma in both children and adults, and respond to the behavioral, emotional, social, and academic impacts of trauma in ways that do not cause additional harm through re-traumatization (Garcia et al., 2023; SAMHSA, 2023). Zero-tolerance and more reactive approaches that reply on discipline and compliance (Bloom, 2013; Downey & Greco, 2023) tend to revisit past events with an emphasis on what was wrong. Utilizing a solution-focused framework accepts that an event occurred and moves the focus to what needs to change for a more preferred future (O'Hanlon, 2010). The solution-focused approach can be highly effective in helping students and adults who have experienced trauma by emphasizing their strengths and focusing on positive change rather than dwelling extensively on the traumatic event itself. This approach can be particularly helpful in several ways:

1. **Strengths and Resilience Focus**: When a student or adult has experienced trauma, they may feel powerless or overwhelmed. By focusing on their strengths, even small successes, the administrator helps the individual regain a sense of control and confidence. This can be empowering and provide hope, which is essential in the healing process.
2. **Future-Oriented Goals**: Trauma can trap students and adults in a cycle of negative thinking about the past.

The solution-focused approach encourages individuals to envision a preferred future and set small, achievable goals that help move them toward it. This forward-looking perspective helps individuals see that positive changes are possible and achievable, even if the trauma is still affecting them.

3. **Short-Term Outcomes**: The solution-focused approach is designed to be brief, which can make it less intimidating for students and adults. Rather than rehashing painful details of their trauma, individuals are encouraged to think about what has worked well for them in the past and how they can apply those skills to their current situation. This approach can yield faster positive outcomes, which is important for students and adults who may not have long-term access to counseling resources.

4. **Scaling Questions and Progress Tracking**: Using tools like scaling questions helps students and staff reflect on their progress and identify small improvements over time. This helps students and adults see that progress is gradual but possible, reinforcing a sense of growth and resilience in the face of trauma.

5. **Focus on Instances of Success**: By identifying instances of success, or times when the problem isn't happening or is less severe, students and adults can learn what actions or circumstances help them feel better, leading to a sense of agency and an understanding of how they can create more positive moments in their lives.

The ideas above can help you to focus on what will be happening instead of focusing on the problem the student or adult is exhibiting, lessening the negative feelings for you and the other individual. For example, with a solution-focused mindset, you would view a student who is regularly engaging in disruptive behavior in class as one struggling with emotion regulation or who is being triggered by something in the here and now rather than a student who is purposefully defiant or disrespectful. By understanding this, you can proactively calm and support the student in developing coping strategies using the solution-focused approach, which benefit everyone involved.

Below are some steps to take and questions to ask when facing a student or adult who is dysregulated:

- Take a pause to check in with your own state of emotion regulation first (e.g., take a breath and ask yourself "what is happening?" or "what happened to this person?")
- Engage with a steady and consistent tone, body language, and expression
- Validate emotions and feelings that are expressed verbally and non-verbally:
  - "Things are really challenging right now."
  - "I hear how upset you are."
  - "I believe you."
- Communicate support while focusing on strengths and future-oriented goals:
  - "What has helped you keep going?"
  - "How are you managing all of that?"
  - "Given all that is going on, what would be most helpful to you now?"
  - "What do you believe the next step is?"

Staying Emotionally Regulated

Making intentional decisions about solution-focused language and action steps that are informed by a trauma-informed "what happened to you?" paradigm are biologically challenging—if not impossible—when we are dysregulated. Therefore, administrators need to take intentional steps to promote emotion regulation before engaging with others using solution-focused approaches. Remember, when we become emotionally dysregulated due to stress, overwhelm, or trauma, the parts of our brain responsible for executive functioning, empathy, and communication go offline (Perry & Winfrey, 2021). Put simply, an emotionally regulated administrator has the capacity to calm a dysregulated student, staff, or family member simply by their regulated presence. An emotionally dysregulated administrator, however, cannot regulate a dysregulated person (Info NMN, 2020). You need to take steps to be mindful of your own state of regulation/dysregulation and to engage in even small moments of self-awareness, movement, and grounding strategies to have full capacity for co-regulation, empathy, and intentional language use to neutralize the environment.

Neutralizing the Environment: Five Guiding Values and Principles

The goal of being trauma-informed is to *neutralize the environment*. In other words, doing things in a way that reduces the likelihood that students, families, and staff experience re-traumatization within the school context. Administrators who are familiar with multi-tiered systems of support (MTSS) can think of being trauma-informed as implementing tier one strategies for school culture and climate based on the knowledge that trauma and adversity are prevalent in the school community. Again, you do not need to know which students, families, and/or staff have trauma, nor do you need to be responsible for treating trauma. Being trauma-informed results in intentional decisions and engagement with students, families, and staff in ways that lessen the chance of making it worse.

The five trauma-informed guiding values and principles are safety, trustworthiness, choice, collaboration, and empowerment (Harris & Fallot, 2001). When integrated with considerations of diversity, equity, inclusion, and accessibility (DEIA), they provide a framework for administrators to engage in universal precaution for trauma within the context of their role. Table 5.4

TABLE 5.4

Solution-Focused Language to Create Trauma-Informed Experiences

Safety: Administrators promote safety by considering the physical and emotional well-being of all members of the school community. This involves considerations of the physical appearance and accessibility of all parts of the school building, being mindful of non-verbal communication (e.g., tone, facial expression proximity), and interacting with others in ways that promote connection.

LANGUAGE FOR ADULTS	LANGUAGE FOR YOUTH
Validation/Acknowledgement	**Validation/Acknowledgement**
Things are really challenging right now.	*I hear that you are angry about this.*
I hear how upset you are.	*I understand you see it differently.*
Coping Questions	**Coping Questions**
How do you get from one moment to the next?	*What helps you get through this?*
What are you doing to take care of yourself even just a little bit in this situation?	*What helps you feel better?*
What is the most important thing for you to remember to continue to cope?	*You must have a good reason for … tell me about it.*
Goal-Formation Questions	**Goal-Formation Questions**
Given all that is going on, what would be most helpful to you now?	*When this problem is solved, what will be different for you?*
Imagine that you leave here feeling that this was useful for you, what would we have talked about?	*What might make sense for us to talk about?*
How might our time together make a difference for you?	*What do you imagine your teacher/parents want to be different about this?*

(Continued)

TABLE 5.4 (Continued)

Trustworthiness: Administrators promote trustworthiness by prioritizing transparent, consistent, and clear communication. This involves letting others know what to expect and what is expected of them, following through on what you say you will do, and expressing patience and acceptance of others' experiences in your interactions.

LANGUAGE FOR ADULTS	LANGUAGE FOR YOUTH
Solution Talk	**Solution Talk**
What is going well?	*What are you good at?*
When things are better, what will be different for you?	*What would your best friend say you are good at?*
What do you believe the next step is?	*What do you think is the most useful thing you could do right now?*
Coping Questions	**Coping Questions**
So tell me ... how do you keep going?	*How did you know that talking to me would be helpful?*
How have you managed to prevent it from getting worse?	*How have your friends been helpful to you?*
Who has noticed the effort you are making?	*How did you manage to keep things together all morning?*
Scaling Questions	**Scaling Questions**
On a scale from 1 to 10 where 10 is you're managing the best you can and 1 is the opposite, where are you?	*On a scale from 1 to 10 where 10 is you believe I can be helpful to you and 1 is the opposite, where are you?*
What are you doing to stay at this number?	*What makes it a (number)?*
What will be different when you move up 1 point higher?	*When you are a little bit higher on the scale what will we be talking about?*
Where would your class put you on this scale?	*On a scale from 1 to 10 where 10 is you are hopeful that things will get better and 1 is the opposite, where are you?*

(Continued)

TABLE 5.4 (Continued)

Choice: Administrators model choice by prioritizing the voice and preferences of the school community when making decisions (even within defined parameters). This involves asking about the preferred future/next steps, exploring what options are available, and ultimately respecting the person's right to choose.

LANGUAGE FOR ADULTS	LANGUAGE FOR YOUTH
Goal Formation Questions	**Goal Formation Questions**
What will be most helpful right now?	*What will be better for you when the problem is solved?*
What are your best hopes in the situation?	*What will you be doing instead of skipping class?*
When you are not doing the problem, what will you be doing instead?	*Suppose things got better, how would you know?*
Difference Questions	**Difference Questions**
What difference will doing (the goal) make?	*When you are back on track, what difference will it make to you?*
What difference will doing (the goal) make for others?	*What difference will it make to your friends when you are no longer in trouble?*
What difference does it make to others that you are working on this?	*What difference will it make to your teacher/coach/parents when you care more?*
Instances of Success Questions	**Instances of Success Questions**
What have you already tried that's been helpful, even if only a little?	*Tell me how you were able to keep on track before?*
What is already working?	*When you were going to class and doing your work, what was better?*
How can you make that happen more often?	*Tell me more about how you tried avoiding the problematic behavior.*

(Continued)

TABLE 5.4 (Continued)

Collaboration: Administrators embody collaboration by treating members of the school community as experts in their own roles and experience. This involves seeking out and exploring the perspective of others to inform solutions and next steps rather than deciding or doing it for them.

LANGUAGE FOR ADULTS	LANGUAGE FOR YOUTH
Goal-Formation Questions	**Goal-Formation Questions**
What are your best hopes for our meeting?	*What would your teacher say needs to change for things to get better?*
How will you and your team know that you've reached your goal?	*What part of that do you agree with?*
What will be the first thing that tells you and your team things are better?	*How do you see what needs to change?*
Instances of Success Questions	**Instances of Success Questions**
What have you and your team already tried, and which of those things helped, if even only a little?	*When things improved before, who was helpful to you?*
What is already working as a team?	*How did you know to listen to them and to take their advice?*
How can you make that happen more often?	*What do you think they would say now that would be helpful to you?*
When are you most supportive of one another?	*When have you found yourself feeling hopeful about this?*
Scaling Questions	**Scaling Questions**
On a scale from 1 to 10 where 10 is we are confident things will improve and 1 is the opposite, where are we?	*On a scale from 1 to 10 where 10 is you are sure things will get better and 1 is the opposite, where are you?*
What are we doing that is making it a #?	*Who is the first person who will notice you moving up on the scale?*
When we move up just a little bit what will each of us be doing that we are not doing now?	*What will they notice?*
Where does it make sense to start?	*When they notice you doing that, what difference will that make to you?*

(Continued)

TABLE 5.4 (Continued)

Empowerment: Administrators prioritize empowerment by noticing and building on strengths, capacities, and previous successes related to the individual, family/team, or situation. This involves asking about what is already working, engaging in ways that are validating and affirming, and highlighting information that can help build a realistic sense of hope.

LANGUAGE FOR ADULTS	LANGUAGE FOR YOUTH
Competency Questions	**Competency Questions**
Tell me something you have been successful with?	What is something you are good at?
What qualities go into doing that?	How did you learn to be good at that?
How would others describe your success?	Who else knows you are good at that?
Instances of Success Questions	**Instances of Success Questions**
When the problem isn't happening, what is?	Tell me about the last time you made a good decision.
How have you made that happen?	What was different about that time?
What else have you done to keep the problem at bay?	When things are better, what do you like about yourself?
Relationship Questions	**Relationship Questions**
What are others noticing that you are doing to get through this?	What might your bestie tell me they like about you?
What might others tell me you are doing to manage that you wouldn't bother telling me?	When you are able to calm yourself, what do others notice about you?
What do others appreciate about you during this time?	When things are better, who usually is the first to notice? What do they notice?

defines each of the values and principles and provides examples of how you can use solution-focused language to create experiences that neutralize trauma reactions and create space for resilience and growth.

Solution-focused questions can be thought of as the "how" to create the "what" of trauma-informed values and principles

(Krause et al., 2017). In the skill examples provided below, solution-focused language enables you to observe past experiences while redirecting attention toward positive aspects or desired changes. This shift in focus serves to mitigate the risk of re-traumatization by avoiding exploration of someone's trauma history, thereby minimizing the potential for eliciting negative emotions and thoughts, particularly when such exploration falls beyond your designated role (Krause et al., 2017).

Case Scenario

A rural high school was impacted by a tragic car accident that killed three students over the summer break. At the start of the school year, several students began to experience challenges with sustaining attention, engaging in meaningful discussions, and participating in usual activities. Teachers had increased sick days, and the school climate was impacted by lower attendance at events and fewer volunteers for activities. The administrator, who was new to the school and district, asked to meet with her key staff and lead teachers in the high school. She explained that the meeting was about how the school was coping with the tragedy that occurred over the summer.

Administrator: Thank you for making time to meet with me on such short notice. I know you all have a lot going on right now. As I mentioned in my email, I want to talk about how the school is managing in the wake of the horrible tragedy this summer. As we all know, I am new here and an outsider. Several of you have had individual conversations with me, and I appreciate how you have tried to help me transition into my role. You all have experienced a terrible loss, as has everyone in the school and community. [silence]

Administrator: I hope it is okay if we start out by me asking you what your best hopes are for this meeting today.

Lead Teacher #1: To be honest I wasn't sure what to expect here.

Guidance Counselor: I think we need a plan and we need to be on the same page.

School Counselor: I am feeling pretty burned out already. Between the parents who are worried about their kids and the kids who are asking to see me, I just have too much. I am hoping we can get some help. Everyone is like a zombie.

[Heads nod]

Lead Teacher #2: I want you to know we are trying to keep it together and do our jobs. I am not sure whether to bring it up or to not bring it up.

Administrator: You all are managing so much with this. What do you imagine would be helpful for us to talk about right now?

Assistant: I think we need to do something as a school community. I know we talked about this already, and I think we really need to do something sooner than later.

[Heads nod]

Lead Teacher #3: Maybe we could try and reach out to that agency [a crisis response team] again to help us. I know they have done this kind of work with other districts.

Administrator: I think it makes sense to ask for outside support, and I wonder what difference it will make to bring people together at this point.

School Counselor: Well, it will give us permission to talk about it openly. I know for me, I would feel supported. We have to be ready for some pretty strong emotions.

Assistant: I know you [administrator] don't know the families, but someone is going to have to reach out to them.

Administrator: Yes, there will be several parts to this [directed to Assistant]. How do you hope doing something as a school community will help?

Assistant: The school is so central to this community, and we all know each other and all of us are, I mean were, connected to those kids…

Administrator: [Nods and waits]
Lead Teacher #1: Let's face it, every day we feel it. The students feel it, the teachers, we need a way to heal...
Administrator: It is a lot for everyone to manage. What else might help?

The administrator continues the meeting acknowledging the pain and sadness while talking about the next steps and how those will be helpful. The administrator in this scenario was torn between wanting to develop the plan and move ahead and attending to the emotions in the room. By staying emotionally regulated herself, she was able to be attentive to the feelings of others while focusing on how they are managing and what they think the next best step is. Further, by doing so, she promoted emotional safety, created space for collaboration, and worked toward building a realistic sense of hope.

Here is a list of the administrator's actions (with the principles of Trauma-Informed Care noted):

1. Recognized the impact of the tragedy on the school community and called for a meeting (Emotional Safety, Collaboration)
2. Alerted the key staff to what the meeting was about (Trustworthiness)
3. Began the meeting by acknowledging the event and impact of the event while also thanking them for their support of her in her role (Emotional Safety, Collaboration)
4. Asked the staff what their goals (best hopes) for the meeting were (Choice)
5. Validated their experiences and stayed with the goal question of helpfulness (Choice, Emotional Safety)
6. Offered agreement and asked about the details of outcomes using difference question (Trustworthiness, Collaboration)

7. Acknowledged ideas and stuck with specific details of outcome (Emotional Safety, Choice)
8. Allowed for the group to do the work by being silent (Empowerment)
9. Validated and asked for more ideas (Emotional Safety, Collaboration, Empowerment)

In this case, the leadership team created a plan to contact a local agency for help. They outlined short- and long-term steps which included contacting the families of the deceased, creating messaging to the larger school community, and holding both community and school-based remembrances. Additional counseling staff was made available for everyone in the school on a short-term basis. This case illustrates that through intentional communication and proactive support, you can create environments that facilitate emotional regulation, promote healing, and cultivate a sense of hope and belonging within your school community.

Using the solution-focused approach and integrating it within trauma-informed programs has the potential to not only assist students or other adults in a school to manage their emotions if triggered but also provide a personal plan of action for the administrator, caught up in a critical situation. By using the steps in this chapter, administrators will find preparation for future events possible and take action during such an event more automatically.

Solution-Focused, Trauma-Informed Sentence Stems for Talking with Students (Reproducible)[1]

- *I understand that you have strong feelings about this. What do you imagine would be helpful for us to talk about right now?*
- *How did you know that talking to me might be helpful?*
- *I understand that this may be difficult to talk about. What do you think is most important for me to know?*
- *I know this is hard. What are your best hopes for this situation?*
- *How do you hope [insert person's ideas] will help? I wonder what difference it will make for you if that happens.*
- *Suppose things got better—How would you know?*
- *What has been helpful to you in managing this so far?*
- *Who has been helpful to you in managing—what have they done that helped?*
- *When things are better, what do you like about yourself?*
- *What do you think is the most useful thing you could do right now? I wonder what your teacher/coach/parents might notice if you did that.*

Chapter Tips for Administrators

Validate [Safety]: Witness and acknowledge feelings. "*I know this is hard.*" "*Things are really frustrating right now.*"

Provide Support and Encouragement [Safety]: To individuals who may be struggling. Use language that conveys empathy, understanding, and belief in their ability to overcome challenges and succeed.

Suspend Judgment [Trustworthiness]: Focus on what has happened rather than what is wrong. Assume people are doing the best they can to manage.

Identify and Build on Signs of Success [Empowerment]: Look for what has been working. Be curious as to how things are not worse.

Set Positive Expectations [Trustworthiness]: Communicate a belief in the potential of all members of the school community. Use language that conveys confidence, optimism, and expectations for success.

Focus on Strengths [Empowerment]: Actively seek out and highlight the strengths, talents, and accomplishments of individuals within the school community.

Ask Future-Oriented Questions [Choice]: What are you working toward? What are the best hopes for the situation? How will you know when this is achieved?

Celebrate Progress [Empowerment]: Celebrate progress and successes, no matter how small. Acknowledge and appreciate the efforts and achievements of students, staff, and stakeholders and use language that reinforces a sense of pride and belonging.

Promote Collaborative Solution Building [Collaboration]: Encourage collaborative solution building by inviting input and ideas from all members of the school community. Use language that fosters a sense of ownership, shared responsibility, and collective efficacy.

Model Solution-Focused Language [All Values/Principles]: Lead by example and model solution-focused language in your interactions with students, staff, and stakeholders. Demonstrate the power of positive communication through your words, actions, and attitudes.

Note

1. See Tables 5.3 and 5.4 for more sentence stems.

References

Bloom, S. L. (2013). *Creating sanctuary: Toward the evolution of sane societies*. Routledge.

Bonanno, G. A., Rennicke, C., & Dekel, S. (2005). Self-enhancement among high-exposure survivors of the September 11th terrorist attack: Resilience or social maladjustment? *Journal of Personality and Social Psychology, 8*(6), 984–998. http://dx.doi.org/10.1037/0022-3514.88.6.984

Byrd-Craven, J., Geary, D. C., Rose, A. J., & Ponzi, D. (2008). Co-ruminating increases stress hormone levels in women. *Hormones and Behavior, 53*, 489–492. https://doi.org/10.1016/j.yhbeh.2007.12.002

Davis, W., Petrovic, L., Whalen, K., Danna, L., Zeigler, K., Brewton, A., Joseph, M., Baker, C. N., & Overstreet, S. (2022). Centering trauma-informed approaches in schools within a social justice framework. *Psychology in Schools, 59*, 2453–2470. https://doi.org/10.1002/pits.22664

Downey, J., & Greco, J. (2023). Trauma sensitive schools: A comprehensive guide for the assessment planning and implementation of trauma informed frameworks. *Children and Youth Services Review, 149*, 106930. https://doi.org/10.1016/j.childyouth.2023.106930

Duane, A. (2023). "Showing the good and bad together": A participatory exploration of strengths and school-based trauma with black elementary youth. *Urban Education*, 1–32. https://doi.org/10.1177/00420859231175673

Ellis, W. R., & Dietz, W. H. (2017). A new framework for addressing adverse childhood and community experiences: The building community resilience model. *Academic Pediatrics, 17*(7), S86–S93. https://doi.org/10.1016/j.acap.2016.12.011

Garcia, A., Sprang, G., & Clemans, T. (2023). The role of school leaders in cultivating a trauma-informed school climate. *Children and Youth Services Review, 146*, 106816. https://doi.org/10.1016/j.childyouth.2023.106816

Harris, M., & Fallot, R. D. (Eds.) (2001). *Using trauma theory to design service systems. New directions for mental health services.* Jossey-Bass.

Herrenkohl, T. I., Hong, S., & Verbrugge, B. (2019). Trauma-informed programs based in schools: Linking concepts to practices and assessing the evidence. *American Journal of Community Psychology, 64*, 373–388. https://doi.org/10.1002/ajcp.12362

Info NMN. (2020, March 30). *3. Emotional contagion: Neurosequential network stress & trauma series* [Video]. YouTube. https://youtu.be/96evhMPcY2Y?si=plEHvx_KiBRnEJ7u

Jennings, A. (2009). *Models for developing trauma-informed behavioral health systems and trauma-specific services: 2008 update*. National Center for Trauma-Informed Care. http://www.theannainstitute.org/Models%20for%20Developing%20Traums-Report%201-09-09%20_FINAL_.pdf

Kim, J. S., Kelly, M. S., & Franklin, C. (2017). SFBT techniques and solution building. In *Solution-focused brief therapy in schools: A 360-degree view of the research and practice principles* (2nd ed., pp. 12–30). Oxford University Press.

Koury, S. P., Green, S. A., & Way, I. (2022). *Trauma-informed organizational change manual*. Institute on Trauma and Trauma-Informed Care. http://socialwork.buffalo.edu/trauma-manual

Krause, D. J., Green, S. A., Koury, S. P., & Hales, T. W. (2017). Solution-focused trauma-informed care (SF-TIC): An integration of models. *Journal of Public Child Welfare*. http://dx.doi.org/10.1080/15548732.2017.1348312

Lê-Cherban, F., Wang, X., Boyle-Steed, K. H., & Pachter, L. M. (2018). Intergenerational associations of parent adverse childhood experiences and child health outcomes. *Pediatrics, 141*(6). https://doi.org/10.1542/peds.2017-4274

MacLochlainn, J., Kirby, K., McFadden, P., & Mallett, J. (2022). An evaluation of whole-school trauma-informed training intervention among post-primary school personnel: A mixed-methods study. *Journal of Child & Adolescent Trauma, 15*, 925–941. https://doi.org/10.1007/s40653-021-00432-3

National Child Traumatic Stress Network. (2008). *Trauma facts for educators*. Author. https://www.nctsn.org/resources/trauma-facts-educators

National Child Traumatic Stress Network. (2022). *Supporting trauma-informed schools to keep students in the classroom: Brief 1. A focus on trauma-informed practices*. https://www.nctsn.org/resources/

supporting-trauma-informed-schools-to-keep-students-in-the-classroom

O'Hanlon, B. (2010). *Quick steps to resolving trauma*. W.W. Norton & Company.

Perry, B. D., & Winfrey, O. (2021). *What happened to you?: Conversations on trauma, resilience, and healing*. Flatiron Books.

Siegel, D. J. (2010). *Mindsight: The new science of personal transformation*. Bantam.

Sprang, G., & Garcia, A. (2022). An investigation of secondary traumatic stress and trauma-informed care utilization in school personnel. *Journal of Child & Adolescent Trauma, 15*, 1095–1103. https://doi.org/10.1007/s40653-022-00465-2

Substance Abuse and Mental Health Services Administration. (2023). *Practical guide for implementing a trauma-informed approach*. https://store.samhsa.gov/sites/default/files/pep23-06-05-005.pdf

Tedeschi, R. G., Shakespeare-Finch, J., Taku, K., & Calhoun, L. G. (2018). *Posttraumatic growth: Theory, research, and applications*. Routledge.

van der Kolk, B. A. (2015). *The body keeps the score: Brain, mind, and body in the healing of trauma*. Penguin Books.

6

Lessening Frequent Flyer Student Returns and Student Discipline Referrals

Linda Metcalf

The same student is in your office once again. The last time she was in your office was Monday and today is Friday. There are two ways to think about this dilemma:

1. What did she do this time?
2. How is it that she was not in my office on Tuesday, Wednesday, and Thursday?

In keeping with the theory behind this book, the second solution-focused question is the most useful. Chances are, asking what she did to be referred would result in more negative conversation which, in the past, has not worked to help the student behave more responsibly. What if, instead, the conversation below happens:

Admin: So, Sarah, my question this afternoon is one of curiosity. I saw you on Monday this week and on Tuesday, Wednesday and Thursday, I did not see you.

Tell me, what were you doing on those days this week to keep yourself from being referred?

No doubt, Sarah will not be used to such a question, so remain curious and do not suggest anything that she might have done. Instead, keep looking at her and sharing that you will wait for her answer, as that answer shows you that she knows what to do in class! Act excited, if possible. Keep waiting, and it is likely that she will come up with something to tell you. But wait, don't settle for one answer—get two or three! Her answers are the most important information on how you can proceed to be the most effective. The more answers you get from Sarah, the more she will recognize that she is competent to avoid referrals, and as a result, can avoid them. Consider, then, what action you need to take according to policy. By waiting until this point, and asking different sorts of questions like those discussed above, Sarah is more likely to understand the action, especially when you add after the action:

I look forward to seeing you in the hallways over the next day or two, as you show me and your teachers more of what you did on Tuesday, Wednesday and Thursday. Let's go over those ideas of yours again before you leave. Then, I will walk you back to class.

What? Walk her back? Yes! By walking her back to class and talking about anything else but what just occurred, you will build a relationship with Sarah. Plus, when you get to her classroom and knock on the door, the teacher will see you and Sarah together where you can solidify the intervention even more by saying:

Thanks, Ms. Montgomery for referring Sarah. She and I have talked, and Sarah is going to try out some new ideas in class today. Would you please watch what she does?

Look at Sarah and say:

Thanks, Sarah, I look forward to hearing what you do.

By taking the extra steps described above, most administrators find a huge decrease in the "frequent flyers" who frequent their offices on a regular basis for the same situations. That's because the teacher is involved in the plan and the student comes up with the strategies. This chapter proposes a different way of thinking about managing students. It is a chapter to rethink how we respond to students who misbehave, frighten us, and act out. It proposes creating a different, solution-focused climate in our schools that can, systemically, begin to make a difference.

Discipline, What's the Point?

Nick Burkett was an administrator in a South African School, called the School of Merit, a school that saw itself as being a solution-focused school. Every teacher, counselor, administrator, secretary, bus driver, cafeteria worker, and janitor was trained to notice the "instances of success" that you see throughout this book. By doing so, not only were the staff more prone to compliment students who tended to frequent the administration office but they were also likely to instill a belief in the students that they were loveable and capable of success. As a result, discipline issues in Nick's school were rare. Yet most of the students in his school would have been considered at risk by American standards. When asked about discipline, he often responded with "Discipline, what's the point, anyway?" (personal communication, 2023). Nick saw discipline as a way of reconnecting with students so they recognized what they needed to do rather than banning them from activities that they probably needed. Sure, they got a consequence, but that was a fraction of the conversation. The rest of their time was spent identifying times and places (including whose classrooms) where they did well. As a result, the students felt he liked them and he did. As a result, the students he saw rarely reoffended.

In the Austin Independent School District, Gonzalo Garza High School is an alternative high school for at-risk students. Eighty percent of its students are considered at risk for not graduating, yet 80% do graduate. Most of the students, when asked about Garza, cited not liking their previous school, and particularly not liking teachers or administrators, as a reason for changing schools. Sixty-five percent of the students mentioned that their relationship with the teachers was the primary difference between Garza and their prior high school. They revealed that because Garza's teachers seemed to care about them and were patient and had higher expectations, they worked for them. One student shared:

> For a quick example, I was incarcerated. All these teachers, they came for me. They had my work ready. One of my teachers even drove to the juvenile hall to give me my homework. What kind of school would do that for its students? Most schools would just look at you and say, 'Obviously you haven't learned your lesson. You're not the kind of students that we need here.' But here (at Garza) they say, 'We still see good in this kid. He may have done bad things but haven't we all.' And when I came back, every teacher gave me a hug.

Another Garza student named Jennifer was at home while she was in the final weeks of her pregnancy, not able to attend school. Jennifer stated:

> On Homebound, that's what you go on when you are pregnant, they bring the work to you. Over there [at her old traditional public school], they had a teacher, but over here they actually bring the work to you.

Both students recognized these events as core differences between teachers at Garza High School and teachers from their traditional high school. The Garza teachers seemed to enable the students to feel a sense of uniqueness, which made them desire success in that teacher's class, both academically and behaviorally (Franklin et al., 2018, pp. 64–65). The climate at Garza was implemented by the administrator, who not only insisted that a new approach take place with the at-risk students who attended but also followed through consistently in the way she hired staff and dealt with students. As a result, Garza has received numerous international and national awards including recognition from the U.S. Department of Education as one of 40 schools in the country that exemplify the best practices for improving outcomes for at-risk students (https://austinisd.my.site.com/Find/s/school-profile/a174x00000OsyFoAAJ/garza-independence-high-school?language=en_US). This school is further described in Chapter 10.

A Better Conversation: Teacher and Student Together

In many schools, the administrator sees students referred by teachers and is seen as responsible for disciplining the students and getting them back on track. Typically, there are punishments designed to teach the student a lesson or deprive him or her of an event or activity that is important to the student. The idea is always to get the point across that disregarding rules or acting out is not acceptable. How often does that work for you, as an administrator? How often do you still see the same students no matter what you assign as their punishment? And even worse, how often do students respond to you with "I don't care." You might grumble when they leave the office that you should not work harder than they do. That makes sense. But there is something else you can try where you can really work less. You can talk to both teacher and student together.

When the teacher is left out of a conversation aiming to correct what a student has done, the chance of a successful outcome decreases dramatically. No matter how hard you try to reach the student and provide the consequence, even with encouragement, when the student returns to the class, the teacher may still see the student as the problem and continue reacting to the student as he/she did before. Thus, the problem will reoccur. This cycle can easily negate your work with the student and result in more non-compliance with the student. Thus, you have *frequent fliers*, or students who frequent your office consistently with referrals.

Most of us have heard that it is important for teachers to build relationships with students, but that does not always happen. Some teachers are reluctant to reach out to the challenging students in any way except in a punitive manner. They get so focused on the misbehavior that they don't notice better behavior. As a result, for those students, the tendency to reoffend the teacher is a natural response. But other teachers have come to learn that talking to a challenging student and lending their ear to what is happening in the student's life has brought them respect and then compliance. Yet students do not experience such relationships often enough, and as a result, they see no reason to comply. So, imagine the difference that the following scenario might have on a student who was again referred by one teacher for disrespecting her.

Case Scenario

Larry, a fourth-grade student, did not get along with his teacher, Ms. Harriett. Larry would not pay attention and would shout out things at times. The teacher constantly corrected him, was sarcastic to him, and often refused to call on him in class, even when he had a good answer. As a result, he became frustrated and stopped working. Ms. Harriett called his parents who were then upset with the school. Larry would come to school after such calls and be worse. One day, when Ms. Harriett brought Larry to the administrator again, she complained about his actions and began to leave when the administrator asked Ms. Harriett to wait and have a seat. He then sent the secretary to Ms. Harriett's class to monitor the students while the students worked. He promised Ms. Harriett that the conversation they were about to have would only take ten minutes.

Admin: Thanks, Ms. Harriett for staying. I know this is a bit different, but I see you as an important person in Larry's life and your input will be helpful. I would like to start out by asking you how you would like things to be for you and Larry in your classroom.
Ms. H: I want him to behave so I can teach. That's all he must do, and he can't do it.
Admin: Sounds good. So, how would his behaving help you to teach?
Ms. H: Well, I could make sure all my students are learning what I need to teach them. Right now, all I do is correct Larry, and I can't teach the others.
Admin: Okay and Larry, how would you like things to be in your class with Ms. Harriett?
Larry: I don't know. She does not like me, and I can't do anything right.
Admin: So, how would you like things to be instead of that?
Larry: I try, I really do, but even when other kids act out, I am the one she gets on to.
Admin: So, again, how would you like things to be in her class?
Larry: Calmer and not so much yelling at me.
Admin: I see. I wonder what Ms. Harriett might need to see you do so things are calmer, and she yells less?
Larry: I have no idea.
Admin: Ms. Harriett, what might Larry do so things are calmer and to show you that he is trying?
Ms. Harriett: Raise his hand to ask a question and act like he is listening to me.

Admin: Okay, and how would you know that he was listening to you?

Ms. Harriett: I guess he would look at me and not talk to Sue.

Admin: Larry, you are looking at me and Ms. Harriett right now and listening to us. I wonder what is going on in here now.

Larry: I am not being yelled at.

Admin: What is happening instead?

Larry: You are talking to me. Nobody talks to me. My parents never talk; all they do is yell. Even my brother yells at me.

Admin: So, Larry, how would you like things to be in Ms. Harriett's class?

Larry: Just calm, I mean, talk to me like normal.

Admin: I wonder, Larry, what would you be willing to do if Ms. Harriett was willing to talk normal to you in class for today like she is in here?

Larry: I think I could try to behave for real.

Admin: Ms. Harriett, would you be willing to try this out, talking normally to Larry as he shows you that he is trying to behave?

Ms. Harriett: Sure. Larry, I really don't like getting upset with you; I just need you to listen to me.

Larry: Okay.

Admin: Ms. Harriett, what might it do for you when Larry tries to behave?

Ms. Harriett: It would mean so much to me. I would really appreciate it, Larry. I do like you.

This is a conversation that I have had countless times in my school counseling office when students were sent to me after visiting with the administrator, who thought the student needed counseling. Instead of just seeing the student, however, I always brought in the teacher. It was sometimes a tense situation, but the questions that I asked only had to do with one thing, what the teacher and the student wanted to happen. As a result of a ten-minute conversation, we typically found out what each person wanted and collaborated on trying it out for a very short period. As a result, the relationship changed from adversarial to collaborative, and everyone walked out with a short plan. I would follow up the next day and then over a few more days with "what's going better?" usually to hear that things were, in fact, going better. Because the teacher and student were working together rather than on their own, they learned from each other what they each wanted. They also each learned what their part was in obtaining what they wanted.

Any administrator can have this conversation. The steps are below, and a reproducible sheet with sentence stems is provided later in this chapter.

Student/Teacher Referral Conversation Steps
1. Ask what each person's best hopes are. It is important that both tell you what they want versus what they do not want.
2. Ask what would be happening in the classroom when the best hopes begin to happen. It is important to get a clear picture of the best hopes.
3. Ask each person to tell you what they can try out for a very short period.
4. Follow up.

Engaging At-Risk Students in School Activities Increases Success

The previous sections discussed several ways to approach the "frequent fliers" who visit your office in a manner that rebuilds relationships and provides students with confidence. Unfortunately, some students still go too far and break rules which require administrators to firmly set boundaries, often leading to suspension or alternative school. Unfortunately, such actions are a temporary fix, where teachers are rid of the student for a time. Yet, upon return, the students return to the same system that helped to create the problem in the first place.

Engaging Students After Suspensions

It would truly be great if suspensions or alternative school placements did the trick so that when students return from school, they innately know how to act to stay out of trouble. Many such students come back from the experience anticipating negativity due to the actions they created, yet not admitting to having any part in the negativity. As a result, without any change in interaction between the suspended student and staff, the student encounters the same environment and interactions with their teachers, staff, and fellow students. This environment leads those at the home campus to only recall negative descriptions and experiences and see the returning student in the same way as they were prior to suspension. That mindset leads to a sort of prejudice against the student, which can ignite the student once again. But what if a suspended student's return experience was different? What if, upon return, they found they were welcomed back by their administrator as a member of the school, which they are, and had a conversation about how to "stay in school" rather than just be warned to do the right thing? And what if they were required, upon return, to engage in the school community as a means of discovering what belonging to a healthy group felt like? The solution-focused approach of this book promotes doing something different when one strategy fails.

A Mentor Program for Re-Entry

When I was a high school counselor, I was always intrigued that most students did better in alternative schools than they did on their home campus, and I wanted to use those *instances of success* at the alternative school when they returned to the home campus. I started visiting students at the alternative school, where I found several of them to be engaged and respectful and working hard in a climate where teachers also treated them differently. There were strict rules that the students had to abide by to progress toward leaving the alternative school, and they complied. Many students brought up their grades and showed a different version of themselves. I wondered what would happen if home campus teachers received the information on what worked at the alternative school when they returned. So, I created a mentor program that helped to drastically reduce the rate of repeat suspensions by 75% the first year it was in practice. What follows are steps that I developed that worked with faculty. Reproducible forms (Metcalf, 2020, p. 66) referenced in the following steps are available in the appendix.

Solution-Focused Mentor Program
Get Buy-in from the Staff

- Begin by sharing your desire to help teachers conduct their classrooms in a manageable fashion. Support your teachers! Describe the mentoring plan you are establishing to help teachers and students have a better experience when the student returns from suspension or the alternative school. Ask your staff to consider being a mentor. Mention that a mentor simply communicates with a student while he or she is in the alternative school or on suspension (or when the student is back on campus) and then meets with the student upon return for support.

Match the Student with a Staff Member Mentor

- The school counselor is an excellent connection between the suspended student or alternative school and the school when it comes to creating a mentor program. The school counselor or administrator can request that *the Student Information Sheet* be given to the student upon suspension or alternative school placement. The sheet provides information for the mentor to create a written correspondence either by email or regular school mail.
- Once there are mentors, match up the student with a home campus mentor. Then send a copy of the *Student Information Sheet* to the mentor. It may help to provide an envelope for the mentor to use for the initial correspondence, if email is not preferred.

Give the Mentor Program Student Survey to Each Student Who Is Suspended and in the Alternative School

- The survey provides the staff at both the alternative school and the home campus a snapshot of the student's worldview. The survey also provides you with a random sample of what these students are thinking, feeling, and needing from their home campus.
- In addition to giving this survey to students when they enroll in the alternative school, you may also wish to get parental permission at that time for the student to communicate with their assigned teacher mentors on the home campus.

Get Information on What Has Worked with the Student

- When the mentored student is ready to return to the home campus, request that the *Teacher Observation Sheet: Alternative School Success* be completed by each of the alternative school teachers and have it sent to you. Copy the sheet and give it to each classroom teacher or email it to them. This valuable information serves as a way to dispel a previous mindset of the student and provide a fresh view of who the student has become. Ask the student's permission to share information with teachers through email and make sure to share a copy with the student!

Reintroduce the Student at the Home Campus

- Meet with the student and teachers prior to the student going to class on the first day back. This may only be a five-minute meeting, but it can be crucial, especially with students who have reoccurring suspensions. Sending a student back to classrooms where the student caused an issue without your intervention as described here may result in more misbehavior. The best scenario happens when all the teachers and the student see each other as trying to do things differently. Do not leave out this step!

Get Support for the Mentor Program

- Consider notifying the Parent-Teacher Association or other school volunteer organizations about the mentor program and encourage them to donate treats for holidays that you can place in mentors' mailboxes.
- Inquire at local restaurants about a discount for pizza or fast food that you can provide twice each semester at a social gathering for mentors and mentored students.
- T-shirts can be designed by students and a designated day of the week can be Mentor Day.
- Put signs on the doors of mentors saying, designaMentor."

While I was a high school counselor, this Mentor Program led to many students remaining on my campus longer after suspension, and some were not suspended for the rest of the school year. I did a quick survey at the end of the school semester to check on how helpful the mentor program was. Over 75% of the students who were mentored said that the mentor program kept them in school. The socials held on the home campus brought mentors and mentees together; instead of being seen as a problem student, the student was seen as a successful student who had an adult who cared. Watching those socials was one of the most exciting events I had when it came to helping students who were previously suspended to remain in school and begin to succeed. I encourage you to try out these ideas as it will lessen your burnout and frustration and bring back the passion you have inside to help every student. Use the forms that follow and add your school logo to them. Then you will be off and running toward solutions and fewer suspensions.

Sentence Stems for Student and Teacher Conversations (Reproducible)

1. *What are your best hopes for your classroom?*
2. *Suppose you both go back to class and this afternoon goes better. What might I see you doing* (student) *and in response, what might you do* (teacher)?
3. *Tell me times when _____behaves slightly better. What do you appreciate about those times?*
4. *Tell me about other classes where you are not acting up. What is going on there that helps you to behave?*
5. *How do you wish your teachers would see you? How can you begin to do that, so you are not referred for a few days?*
6. *When faced with a teacher who simply wants the student to stop doing an action, ask: what would you like him/her to do instead?*
7. *Share with teachers: I am creating this program (or having this conversation with you and the student) because I want you to have the classroom that helps you to be the best teacher you can be.*

Chapter Tips for Administrators

1. When students are referred to you by their teacher, always include teachers in the conversation to build solutions with the student.
2. When a student is referred again, look for instances of success, or the time in between the referrals. Ask the student how he/she has managed to NOT be referred during those times.
3. When students return from suspension, having a meeting with the teachers and student together improves likelihood that the behaviors decrease.

4. The alternative school successes that a student has should be seen as instances of success. Find out what occurred there that can be done on the home campus.
5. When trying to get a teacher to do something different, remind the teacher that you are focused on him having a classroom where he can be the teacher he wants to be. This will create buy-in.
6. Use the survey to see where the student is regarding feeling successful, cared for, and encouraged. Use the survey to engage teachers to provide more relational interactions that show the student he is cared for.

References

Burkett, N. (2023). Keynote presentation. Solution Focused Schools Unlimited Annual Conference, virtual.

Franklin, C., & Streeter, C. L. (2003). *Creating solution focused accountability schools for the 21st century: A training manual for Garza high school.* The University of Texas at Austin, Hogg Foundation for Mental Health.

Franklin, C., Streeter, C. L., Webb, L., & Guz, S. (2018). *Solution focused brief therapy in alternative schools.* Routledge.

Metcalf, L. (2020). *The solution focused school climate.* KDP Publishers. KDP Publishers.

APPENDIX

The Mentor Program Student Survey

Please answer the following questions as honestly as possible. You do not need to put your name on this paper because it is confidential. No one here at school will know that these are your answers. This survey is designed to help you to help our school improve its services to students.

Use the numbers below to answer the questions. Circle the number that fits your answer:

1 = never,   2 = sometimes,   3 = always

1. I like coming to school. 1 2 3
2. My teachers help me to be the best that I can be. 1 2 3
3. When I am at school, I feel important to my teachers. 1 2 3
4. I feel safe at school. 1 2 3
5. I work well with other students. 1 2 3
6. I have friends that I can depend on. 1 2 3
7. I like who I am. 1 2 3
8. I think I have potential to do well. 1 2 3
9. My family encourages me to do well in school. 1 2 3
10. I think my teachers care about me. 1 2 3

The Mentor Program
Parental Permission Sheet

Date: _____

I, parent of _____, give my permission for him/her to communicate with a faculty mentor while in alternative school during suspension. I understand that all communication is monitored and available to me upon asking for it.

_____

Parent/Guardian

The Mentor Program Student Information Sheet

Dear Student,

While you are away from your home campus, you will have a mentor who will write to you occasionally. The information that you share here will help the mentor get to know you.

Your Name: _____ Grade: _____

Home Campus: _____

Describe your interests, hobbies, and what you like to do outside of school.
_____
_____
_____

What do you hope your alternative school teachers notice about you?
_____
_____
_____

What do you need from your teachers at your home campus when you return?
_____
_____
_____

Thanks for your time.

Copyright material from Marcella D. Stark and Linda Metcalf (eds.) (2025), *Solution-Focused Strategies for K–12 Leaders*, Routledge

Your Mentor Assignment

Dear Student,

Your mentor is _____
While you are at _____ you will receive occasional letters from your mentor, who wants to support you in your efforts to get back on track at school. Your mentor will be someone that you can visit with upon your return to the home campus for support when you need it.

When you receive a letter from your mentor, please respond to your mentor by using the enclosed envelope. Give the envelope to your teacher at the alternative school and ask that it be sent to your home campus.

I wish you well.

_____
School Counselor

Teacher Observation Sheet of Success

Dear Teacher,

Your student, _____, will return to his or her home campus very soon. Your observations of what has been helpful to the student while he/she was in your class will be very important to the home campus teachers. Below, please write down what you have noticed as **helpful** teaching strategies, as well as classroom management strategies that seemed to work with this student.

Teaching Methods That Work

1. _____
2. _____
3. _____
4. _____
5. _____

Description of abilities: Please list positive traits that you observed about this student in your classroom:

_____
_____
_____
_____
_____

_____   _____
Your Signature   Subject /Classroom

7

Working with Students in Crisis

Carol E. Buchholz Holland

In a recent study conducted by the University of Minnesota, Minnesota school principals were surveyed and then asked to identify from a list of 49 leadership activities which activity presented the single greatest challenge to school leaders (Kemper et al., 2024). "Addressing student mental health challenges" was the most commonly selected activity as being the greatest challenge. The study's findings also revealed that the principals believed they possessed the lowest levels of self-efficacy when responding to student mental health challenges. Furthermore, "addressing emergency and crisis situations" were two of the areas identified in the survey findings that administrators felt the least prepared for (Kemper et al., 2024).

Although diagnosing student mental health concerns is not part of a school administrator's training or job description, identifying early warning signs of a student in crisis is an essential task that they should be able to do. Ideally, administrators will work collaboratively with their school's mental health professionals when they encounter a student who is in crisis. However,

DOI: 10.4324/9781003463504-7

sometimes these mental health professionals are not available, so the administrator needs to know how to respond to a student crisis on their own. In addition, it is important for school administrators to know how to talk with students and their families if any student mental health concerns are identified during a meeting. School administrators also need to receive training on how to make a student referral for outside mental health services if they are needed.

Fortunately, there are several evidence-based training programs designed for school administrators which focus on identifying student mental health concerns and responding to students in crisis. Here are some examples:

- *PREPaRE School Crisis Prevention and Intervention Training*: This program was developed by the National Association of School Psychologists (NASP) and is an evidence-based training program that focuses on school crisis prevention and response (https://www.nasponline.org/professional-development/prepare-training-curriculum).
- *Question, Persuade, Refer (QPR) for Suicide Prevention*: QPR is an evidence-based suicide prevention training that equips individuals with the skills to recognize the warning signs of suicide, offer hope, and refer individuals to appropriate help (https://qprinstitute.com/about-qpr).
- *Trauma-Informed Schools Training*: This training focuses on creating trauma-informed school environments, helping administrators understand the effects of trauma on students, and supporting students effectively (https://safesupportivelearning.ed.gov/trauma-sensitive-schools-training-package).
- *Youth Mental Health First Aid (YMHFA)*: This evidence-based program teaches adults how to identify, understand, and respond to signs of mental health challenges in youth (https://www.mentalhealthfirstaid.org/).

In addition to these outside formal trainings, school mental health professionals such as directors of guidance programs, school counselors, psychologists, or social workers within their own school district may be excellent resources who can provide training, leadership, and support in addressing student mental health issues.

Sometimes while meeting with a student for disciplinary reasons, you may discover that the student is experiencing a mental health crisis. Due to rising rates of student mental health concerns and oftentimes overwhelmed school-based mental health services, it is becoming more common that school administrators need to intervene and provide support to students when they are in crisis (Kemper et al., 2024). However, you may only have limited training or no training at all on how to effectively respond to a student crisis. Furthermore, you may not be fully confident about how to address serious mental health concerns such as suicidal ideation.

Understanding Crises and Responding with a Not Knowing Stance

James (2008) defined "crisis" as "a perception or experiencing of an event or situation as an intolerable difficulty that exceeds the person's current resources and coping mechanisms" (p. 3). During a crisis, formerly successful coping mechanisms fail because they cannot provide sufficient support for dealing with the current crisis situation. As a result, a person in crisis may feel a wide range of emotions such as hopelessness, helplessness, confusion, anxiousness, anger, or vulnerability. The Centers for Disease Control and Prevention (CDC) recently released the CDC Youth Risk Behavior Survey: Data Summary & Trends Report 2011–2021, and the report indicates that students' experiences with violence, mental health, and suicidal thoughts and behaviors worsened significantly between 2011 and 2021 (CDC, n.d.).

Youth behavioral problems which may occur at school and/or at home are also commonly linked with other mental health conditions (e.g., anxiety, depression) (Ghandour et al., 2019). Although it is difficult to know for certain the full impact that mental health diagnoses may have on student behavior, it is recommended you take these diagnoses into consideration during disciplinary meetings with students and when determining how to respond. However, you may or may not be aware of a student's diagnosis when you meet with the student. Because of this, it is helpful to take a solution-focused "not knowing" stance when you begin your meeting with the student. By taking a "not knowing" stance, you can help de-escalate tense situations and identify potential solutions by:

1. **Asking open-ended questions**: Asking open-ended questions will encourage the student to share their thoughts, feelings, and experiences without you leading the conversation.
   Example: *Can you tell me about what brought you here today from Ms. Minton's class?*
2. **Avoiding making assumptions**: Avoid making assumptions about the reasons behind the student's behavior or challenges. Instead of presuming to know why something happened, invite the student to explain it in their own words.
   Example: *How would you rather things be in Ms. Minton's class?*
3. **Using active listening skills**: Listen attentively without interrupting or jumping to conclusions. Reflect back on what you hear to ensure understanding and use the student's own words as much as possible.
   Example: *So, instead of being overwhelmed (or answer to previous question), you would rather get your homework done so you could stay in after-school activities ... is that correct?*

4. **Maintaining curiosity**: Maintain a curious and open attitude throughout the conversation and continuously explore the student's perspective without jumping to conclusions.
   Examples: *Tell me about other times when you were overwhelmed and you managed your school work and were able to stay in an activity. How might those coping strategies be helpful to you now?*
5. **Focusing on the student's strengths and resources**: Help the student identify their strengths, past successes, and available resources that can be applied to their current challenge.
   Example: *Tell me about a time when you handled a difficult situation well. What did you do that worked? What else?*
6. **Collaborating to identify solutions**: Work with the student to co-create solutions instead of telling the student what should be done. Explore possible strategies together.
   Example: *Let's put your ideas to work—what's one small step you could take that might help improve things a little bit over the next day or two?*

Using a solution-focused "not knowing" stance helps create a safe and respectful space where your student can feel listened to and valued. By focusing on understanding the student's perspective and collaborating on solutions, you can help the student tap into their own strengths and resources which can lead to more effective outcomes.

Possible Warning Signs of a Student in Crisis

As mentioned earlier, it is important that you are able to identify potential warning signs of a student in crisis. Students who need additional assistance may exhibit a range of signs and behaviors indicating severe distress or an inability to cope with their current circumstances. Recognizing these signs is crucial for timely intervention and support. Here are some examples of common indicators:

Emotional Signs
- Persistent or extreme sadness, tearfulness, or feelings of hopelessness
- Anxiety, excessive fear, or panic attacks
- Sudden mood swings
- Increased anger or irritability

Behavioral Signs
- Withdrawal from friends, family, or school/social activities
- Increased isolation and desire to be left alone
- Changes in academic performance such as a sudden decline in academic performance, lack of interest in schoolwork, or skipping classes
- Being disruptive in class such as displaying aggression, hostility, or violence
- Engaging in risky behaviors
- Substance abuse
- Writing, talking, or drawing about death and dying

Physical Signs
- Changes in appearance such as neglect of personal hygiene or appearance; or noticeable weight loss or gain
- Sleep disturbances such as insomnia or excessive sleeping

Cognitive Signs (North Dakota Health & Human Services, n.d.; Ryan & Oquendo, 2020; SAMHSA, 2012)
- Difficulty concentrating on tasks or following through with responsibilities
- Frequent forgetfulness or indecisiveness

In addition to the warning signs listed above, students experiencing suicidal ideation may share **verbal cues** such as (National Institute of Mental Health, n.d.; North Dakota Health & Human Services, n.d.):

- Making statements like "What's the point of living anymore?" or "Things will never get better."
- Expressing feelings of hopelessness or helplessness
- Sharing feelings of worthlessness, guilt, or self-blame
- Talking about being a burden to others
- Saying goodbye to friends and family as if for the last time
- Talking about death or expressing a desire to die
- Making direct mention of suicidal thoughts or self-harm

By knowing the signs of a crisis in a student, the administrator is more likely to avoid focusing on the problematic behavior and work more on developing an empowering situation.

Case Scenario

You are asked to meet with Jenna, a 16-year-old female student, who stormed out of a classroom today after she refused to put her cell phone away when instructed by her teacher. You are surprised by Jenna's actions because she is known for her friendly demeanor and academic achievements. However, when Jenna first walks into your office, she looks like she had been crying, and her appearance is a little disheveled which is not typical for her. In addition, she seems to be agitated and visibly upset. You quickly get a sense that there might be more going on with Jenna than just this discipline issue.

What would you do?

This scenario helps illustrate how the solution-focused approach can be used to assist students in identifying their coping strategies, resources, and strengths. Furthermore, it can help engage students and increase the likelihood that students will be willing to acknowledge if they are in crisis. Here are some recommended solution-focused steps to take when meeting with a student.

Build Rapport and Ask for a Brief Description of the Student's Concern

The student (Jenna) has been sent to your office because she refused to put her cell phone away and abruptly left her classroom without permission. You notice that she is visibly upset and agitated. When encountering a student who appears to be distressed, it is helpful to initially take the time to build rapport and gain a better understanding of the student's situation. Without rapport, it may be more difficult to develop trust between you and the student, and it may decrease the likelihood that the student would disclose to you if they were actually in crisis.

Demonstrating empathy and respect, taking a non-judgmental attitude, and being an active listener are effective ways to develop rapport with a student during a meeting. As mentioned earlier in this chapter, it is helpful for you to take a "not knowing" stance where you remain in an open, curious, and non-expert position while you interact with Jenna (De Jong & Berg, 2013). You can ask open-ended questions to explore the situation from Jenna's perspective without assuming that you already know the answers. Students are more likely to become engaged and invested in the process if they feel heard and respected.

Here's an example of a solution-focused administrator starting a conversation with Jenna:

Administrator: Jenna, thank you for coming in to meet with me. I'd like to talk with you about what happened in Mr. Radel's class today. I've already read the incident report that he sent to me. However, I would like to understand things from your perspective. Would you please briefly share with me what took place?

Jenna's eyes begin to water a little and she says:

Jenna: I don't know ... I didn't mean to be disrespectful. I just didn't know what else to do.

The administrator notes the subtle signs of distress in Jenna's body language and the tone of her voice which leads the administrator to suspect that Jenna may be upset about more than just being written up and sent to the office.

Administrator: I'm sensing there may be more going on with you than just being written up for using your cell phone. Would I be correct in assuming that?

Jenna takes a long pause. When she finally speaks, her voice is filled with emotion and she says:

Jenna: Yeah ... well, I guess I'm just dealing with a lot right now, and I'm feeling really overwhelmed. When Mr. Radel got on my case for using my cell phone in class, it became too much for me to handle today. Instead of embarrassing myself in front of everyone, I left the classroom before I lost it or started to cry.

Using a gentle and supportive voice, the administrator says:

Administrator: It sounds like you are dealing with a lot right now.

Jenna shifts uncomfortably in her seat, avoids eye contact with the administrator, and then says:

Jenna: Yeah, I guess ... It's just that I've been having a really rough time lately.
Administrator: What would be most helpful for us to talk about today?

By wording the question in this way, the administrator is trying to convey to the student that they are interested in identifying information which would immediately benefit the student instead of spending a lot of time focusing on the causes of the student's problems (Fiske, 2008).

Jenna: Ever since my parents divorced, my mom has been putting a lot of pressure on me to be the perfect daughter and student. That's really caused my anxiety to really get out of control at times. I feel so overwhelmed at times.

Administrator: Jenna, I appreciate you sharing this information with me. I know that it isn't always easy to talk about the times when we struggle.

Engage in a Coping Dialogue

After the student shares brief details about their challenges and the administrator acknowledges them, the student is prompted to engage in a *coping dialogue*. The coping dialogue is an essential part of solution-focused conversations and interventions. It also helps build hope because it can increase a student's sense of agency and expand the number of pathways they can use to cope with a problem. Unlike a problem-focused practitioner who may jump right into assessing the student's problems and gathering as many details about the problems as possible, a solution-focused practitioner encourages the student to engage in a coping dialogue which assists the student in identifying, utilizing, and building upon their existing coping strategies and strengths in order to help manage current difficulties that they are experiencing. In addition to being asked about current coping strategies, the student is asked about strategies that have worked for them in the past. The student is encouraged to apply these strategies or skills to their current problem. Key elements of a solution-focused coping dialogue include emphasizing the student's past successes, resources, and strengths. The administrator demonstrates active listening skills by reflecting on what the student briefly shared with them about their current situation and encourages the student to begin identifying coping strategies that they have been using.

Administrator: It sounds like you've been going through a lot lately. How have you been coping with this situation so far?" or "What have you been doing lately that has been helping even a little bit?

Jenna: When I'm at home I like to take my dog for a long walk or go for a bike ride.

Administrator: What have you found helpful in the past when you've been at school?

Jenna: Well, I guess I try using some deep breathing techniques that my elementary school counselor taught me years ago. That works sometimes.

It is helpful to gather as many rich details about the student's coping strategies and this can be done by asking a simple follow-up question such as "What else?" The administrator can continue to ask the "What else" question until the student can no longer identify any new strategies. If the student to able to share some coping strategies that they have used, the administrator can give the student a "direct compliment" which reinforces the student's positive efforts to cope.

Adminstrator: That's great that you've been using the deep breathing techniques that you learned during a guidance lesson in elementary school. It shows that you want to work on regulating your emotions.

The administrator can also ask additional follow-up strength-based and resource identification questions such as:

Administrator: Which of your personal strengths have helped you deal with challenges in the past? What else?
Who in your life supports you during difficult times? Who else?

Assisting with the identification of past successes is an essential part of the solution-focused process. By highlighting past successes, the student is reminded of their abilities and strengths which can help increase their confidence and sense of agency. In addition, helping the student recall past successes can instill hope and optimism which in turn may increase the likelihood that the student begins to believe that positive change is possible.

Administrator: Can you think of a time when you were successful in managing your anxiety and felt a little more in control?
Jenna: Well, I normally get really anxious when it's time to take tests, especially my finals. However, I was able to calm myself down a little before I took my finals last spring and things turned out ok.
Administrator: Wow, that's great. What did you do to help you manage your anxiety even a little bit?

A follow-up question could be: *"How might you apply those strategies to your current situation?"*

In addition to identifying past successes, it is helpful to ask about times when a problem is less of a problem and the student is a little closer to their ideal. Discussing what was happening during these *instances of success* (George et al., 1999) and what the student was doing that might have contributed to making the situation better can help identify possible coping strategies and solutions.

Administrator: You mentioned that you were able to manage your anxiety a little bit better last spring when you took your finals. What did you do differently during that time that helped you?

Follow-up questions could be: *What might others have noticed you doing then that was helpful?*
What else?

Engaging a student in a coping dialogue can be an effective way to help stabilize the student and help them regulate their emotions. The reason this type of dialogue can be a powerful tool is because it encourages the identification of coping strategies that worked in the past and can be applied to the student's current situation.

Gather Information about the Student's Current Level of Safety

Some students who are in crisis may have difficulty engaging in a coping dialogue. If the administrator notices a student is struggling to identify coping strategies, resources, or past successes, the administrator is encouraged to gather information about the student's current level of safety and ascertain if the student is considering any form of self-harm or experiencing suicidal ideation. It is important to note that the following questions are not intended to determine a formal threat or risk level. Instead, the information gathered will be used later on to help the student create a safety plan. However, before asking the student a question about their current level of safety, it is recommended that the administrator first normalize this question. For example, the administrator may say:

Administrator: Whenever I meet with a student who seems to be struggling or dealing with tough issues, I ask them about how safe they feel and if they have had any thoughts about hurting themselves. I realize that when people are really hurting or are feeling overwhelmed by their problems, they may have thoughts of hurting themselves from time to time (Henden, 2008). The reason I ask these questions is because I want to help keep students safe and help them find alternative ways to deal with their problems.

Adminstrator: So I'm wondering ... have you had any thoughts of hurting yourself? or Have you had any thoughts of suicide? Have you had any of these thoughts recently?

After asking these questions, it is helpful to follow up with a solution-focused *scaling question* (DeJong & Berg, 2008). This type of question can assist the student with quantifying their thoughts and feelings, and with expressing them in a concrete way without the need for words. Scaling questions can be very useful when gathering information about overwhelming experiences such as suicidal ideation, especially if the student struggles to verbally articulate their emotions. Using a scaling question can also make it easier for the student to communicate their level of distress to the administrator. Whereas many counselors scale the intensity of a student's suicidal thoughts, solution-focused scaling questions typically use a scale from 1 to 10 (or 0 to 10) where the "10" represents the student's preferred future. Therefore, if the student indicates that they have had thoughts of suicide, an administrator may ask the student to scale their feelings of safety, where "10" represents the student feeling completely safe with no suicidal thoughts and "1" represents a strong intention to harm themselves. With this information, the administrator may determine next steps. If the student scales anything lower than 9, they should be referred to the school counselor or other mental health professional for follow-up, and ratings of 3 or lower warrant an immediate action for safety.

The conversation may go something like this:

Administrator: On a scale of 1 to 10, with '10' feeling safe with no thoughts of suicide and 1 representing very intense feelings of suicide, how safe would you say you are feeling right now?
How would you have rated these feelings yesterday (or last week)?

The administrator will then ask the student follow-up questions if the intensity level of their suicidal thoughts has changed over time.

Administrator: You mentioned that your suicidal thoughts are more intense today than it was yesterday. I'm wondering... what was different about yesterday? What were you doing differently? What do you think might have helped you even a little bit to make things a little more bearable for you yesterday?

If it turns out that their suicidal thoughts were less intense yesterday (i.e., they scaled themselves high on feeling safe), the administrator will ask about what small things the student has been doing today that are helping them to feel safe, even a little bit. For example, the administrator may ask:

Administrator: You mentioned that you were at a 5 yesterday and today, you are at a 6. Tell me how <u>confident</u> you are right now that you can remain at a 6 or higher today. What gives you that confidence?

After the student responds to this question, the administrator may ask follow-up questions such as:

Administrator: What are you currently doing to keep the number higher? or What helps keep that number from going lower? or What is the lowest number you have been on that scale? What have you done that has helped that scale be higher so you feel more confident about remaining safe? (Bodmer Lutz, n.d.)

Fiske (2008) also mentioned that "identifying, highlighting, and reinforcing reasons for living" can be a powerful tool to engage people in searching for alternative options to suicide (p. 8). Taking this into consideration, the administrator may explore the student's possible reasons for living by asking:

Administrator: In the past, how have you stopped yourself from acting on your suicidal thoughts? What else?

Asking students to identify their reasons for living may help identify the people (or even pets) who are important to the student and who may also serve as resources for the student. This question can also remind the student about their connections with others which may reduce their feelings of isolation. In addition, if a student is able to identify their reasons for living, these reasons may motivate them to accept additional mental health support.

Connect the Student with a Mental Health Professional and Contact the Student's Parent/Guardian

After engaging the student in a coping dialogue and gathering information about the student's safety level, it is now time to refer the student in crisis to a mental health professional for additional support. You may reach out and help connect the student with a school-based mental health professional. If these professionals are not available or if the student needs immediate or more intensive services, you will need to initiate contact with the student's parent/guardian and will follow your school's guidelines for making a referral for outside mental health services. Talking with the student's parents helps to facilitate a collaborative conversation and encourages the student to play an active role in it. The student will also be asked to share with their parent/guardian the coping strategies, resources, and past successes that they identified with the administrator. However, sharing these strategies, resources, and past successes is not meant to minimize the seriousness of the student's suicidal ideation. Instead, they are used to create a *conversational hope space* which helps to reduce feelings of shame, fear, distrust, hopelessness, and/or helplessness that the parent/guardian may initially feel when they learn about their child's suicidal ideation (Fiske, 2008; Henden, 2008). By sharing this information, the hope is that the student and their parent/guardian will be more likely to accept and engage in mental health services.

In most cases, you will need to contact the student's parent/guardian if the student is experiencing suicidal ideation.

However, if you know or have "reasonable cause to suspect" that the "student has been or is likely to be abused or neglected if/when" their parent/guardian is contacted about the student's suicidal ideation, you are advised to postpone contacting the parent/guardian (Beaverton School District, n.d., Level 1 Suicide Screening). Instead, you would need to make a report to their county or state's Child Protective Services (CPS) office and then follow the CPS recommendations on how to proceed with parent/guardian notification.

Conclusion

A major tenet of the solution-focused approach is: "If it isn't broken, don't fix it. If it works, do more of it. If it's not working, do something different." (de Shazer, 1985, pp. 2–3). Taking this tenet into consideration, you are encouraged to look for things that are working in your schools. Using the solution-focused approach to develop policies and procedures for responding to students in crisis involves capitalizing on the existing strengths, resources, and insights of the school community in order to create effective and supportive strategies. This approach can foster a positive, collaborative, and proactive environment for addressing crises. As an administrator embracing the solution-focused approaches in this book, creating policies to keep your students safe personalizes your students' unique needs and provides your staff with more useful information.

Solution-Focused Actions and Sentence Stems (Reproducible)

Define desired outcomes and goals
- *What are our best hopes for developing these policies and procedures? What outcomes do we hope to achieve?*
- *How do we develop students' protective factors and increase connectedness in our school?*

Describe the school's preferred future
- *What does a successful response to a student in crisis look like in our school?*
- *What will be happening in our school after we have implemented effective policies for assisting students in crisis?*
- *Who will be involved and what will they be doing to help contribute?*

Identify existing strengths and resources
- *What are our school's current strengths and resources that help us respond effectively to students in crisis?*
- *What is currently going well in our school's efforts to support students?*

Learn from past successes
- *Think of a time when you were successful in helping a student in crisis. What did you do that worked well?*
- *What did others do that helped?*

Identify coping strategies
- *What coping strategies and activities have we used in the past that were effective and helped support students in crisis?*
- *What can we provide again?*

Look for instances of success
- *When are times that things are going better in our school?*
- *What is different about those times?*
- *How did we help make that happen?*

Generate practical solutions
- *What steps can we take that will help us improve our school climate and increase our school community's well-being?*
- *What has worked in the past that we can implement again?*

Use scaling questions for assessment purposes
- *On a scale of 1 to 10, with "10" being it was "very useful" and "1" being the opposite, how useful do you believe this crisis response protocol is?*

Develop collaborative plans
- *How can we involve students, teachers, staff, and parents/guardians in developing and implementing new crisis response policies?*
- *What has helped motivate them to get involved in school initiatives in the past?*

Chapter Tips for School Administrators

- **Know the risk factors and warning signs of students in crisis.** Early identification and intervention are key to supporting students.
- **Take all signs of distress seriously** and don't ignore them.
- **Stay calm and present.** Maintaining a calm demeanor helps to de-escalate the situation and provide a sense of stability and safety for the student. Remember that

students are observing you and how you respond to what they share with you.
- **Use empathic and active listening skills** to help understand the student's feelings and their situation without judgment. For example, *"It sounds like you're feeling really overwhelmed right now. Is that correct?"*
- **Build rapport** by showing genuine care and concern.
- **Take a "not knowing" stance** and do not make assumptions about the student or their actions.
- **Engage the student in a coping dialogue** which helps the student identify their coping strategies and promotes the hope-building process.
- **Collaborate with the student to explore potential solutions**, rather than imposing your own ideas.
- **Ask questions which help students identify their strengths, resources, and past successes** in overcoming difficult situations. For example, *"Can you remember a time when you faced something difficult and were able to get through it? What did you do that helped even a little bit?"*
- **Highlight progress—no matter how small—and provide a direct compliment.** It is helpful to recognize any positive changes or efforts that the student has made no matter how small they are. For example, *"You mentioned that you reached out to your biology teacher about your concerns. That's a big step in the right direction."*
- **Ask questions that direct the student's attention toward solutions rather than dwelling on the problem.** For example, *"If things were a little better tomorrow, what would you be doing that you are not doing today?"*
- **Ask direct questions**: Gently but directly ask the student about their feelings and thoughts. For example, *"Are you thinking about hurting yourself?"*

- **Assess for safety** and collaboratively begin developing a safety plan.
- **Identify students' support system** and ask who are the important people in their lives.
- **Acknowledge, validate, and** normalize student's emotional responses.
- **Stay with the student**: Do not leave the student alone if they are expressing suicidal thoughts or severe distress.
- **Make sure they are in a physically safe environment** while you are waiting to get them connected to mental health support.

References

Beaverton School District (n.d.). *Suicide intervention.* https://www.beaverton.k12.or.us/departments/teaching-learning/student-services/social-work/suicide-prevention-plan/suicide-intervention

Bilsen, J. (2018). Suicide and youth: Risk factors. *Frontiers in Psychiatry, 9,* 1–5.

Bodmer Lutz, A. (n.d.). *Cope is one letter away from hope: Solution-Focused Safety Assessment (SFSA).* https://solutionfocused.net/cope-is-one-letter-away-from-hope-solution-focused-safety-assessment-sfsa/

Centers for Disease Control and Prevention (CDC) (n.d.). *Youth Risk Behavior Survey: Data Summary & Trends Report 2011–2021.* https://www.cdc.gov/yrbs/?CDC_AAref_Val=https://www.cdc.gov/healthyyouth/data/yrbs/pdf/yrbs_data-summary-trends report2023_508.pdf

DeJong, P., & Berg, I. K. (2008). *Interviewing for solutions* (3rd ed.). Brooks/Cole.

De Jong, P., & Berg, I. K. (2013). *Interviewing for solutions* (4th ed.). Brooks/Cole.

de Shazer, S. (1985). *Keys to solution in brief therapy.* Norton.

Fiske, H. (2008). *Hope in action: Solution-focused conversations about suicide.* Routledge.

George, E., Iveson, C., & Ratner, H. (1999). *Problem to solution: Brief therapy with individuals and families* (Revised and expanded edition). Brief Therapy Press.

Ghandour, R. M., Sherman, L. J., Vladutiu, C. J., Ali, M. M., Lynch, S. E., Bitsko, R. H., & Blumberg, S. J. (2019). Prevalence and treatment of depression, anxiety, and conduct problems in US children. *The Journal of Pediatrics, 206,* 256–267.

Henden, J. (2008). *Preventing suicide: The solution-focused approach.* John Wiley & Sons.

James, R. K. (2008). *Crisis intervention strategies* (6th ed.). Brooks/Cole.

Kemper, S., Pekel, K., Evenson, A., Seabrook, R., Fynewever, N., & Zhao, Q. (2024). *Report of findings from the second biennial Minnesota principals survey.* Center for Applied Research and Educational Improvement, College of Education and Human Development, University of Minnesota. https://carei.umn.edu/sites/carei/files/2024-04/April-2024-MnPS-2023-main-report.pdf

National Institute of Mental Health (n.d.). *Warning signs of suicide.* https://www.nimh.nih.gov/health/publications/warning-signs-of-suicide

North Dakota Health & Human Services (n.d.). *When should you be concerned about a student?* https://www.hhs.nd.gov/behavioral-health/prevention/suicide/schools/identify

8

Successful Students with Autism and Intellectual Disabilities

Sharon Casey and Jennifer LeHuquet

This chapter outlines how a solution-focused (SF) project implemented at a public high school in Canada for students with autism and intellectual disabilities created significant and lasting changes in case conference meetings, classroom management, and overall school culture. Here you will find practical tips and tools that can be used in any school.

In early 2021, our school district offered training to teachers and administrators on SF practices to address emotional and behavioral difficulties with students. As the principal of a high school for students with cognitive and developmental disabilities, I (JH) had doubts that any mainstream professional development could be applied in our specialized environment. Each of the 100 students in our public high school has a recognized learning disability, intellectual delay, developmental disorder, or other neurodivergence, notably autism. Our programs aim to teach academic, social, and life skills to students aged 11 to 21. Our students do not qualify for a regular high school diploma upon graduation, and all of them are deemed to be at-risk and have shown failure to progress in mainstream schools despite accommodations and individualized education plans. They often have poor self-esteem, and most do not like school. Our team works hard to create a sense of belonging and to help students develop the academic and life skills they need to be successful and productive citizens.

My misgivings about professional development were soon assuaged. As described by our trainer (SC), the SF approach was a radically simple mind shift that resonated deeply with my educational philosophy. I could not wait to share what I had learned with our staff. I could imagine so many applications for this approach to improve our school. It is important to understand that the SF approach is not just for neurotypical students. What we propose in this chapter applies to anyone capable of some degree of self-awareness and communication (though, as you will see, verbal communication is not strictly required).

Laying the Groundwork

When I (JH) returned to school, I called in my leadership team—a staff assistant, school counselor, and lead teacher—to discuss how the SF approach could benefit our school. The leadership team quickly pointed out that the most significant challenge would be unlearning some "bad habits" that are pervasive in most schools, namely, spending most of our time defining problems, searching for examples of problems, and trying to identify the underlying causes of problems.

Before embarking on a plan to change the school culture, it was essential to identify how this change would benefit the staff and students and decide on how to start small and measure progress. In the change management process, defining the first step, the entry point, is most likely to lead to an early "win" and is essential. We decided that we could readily adapt our multidisciplinary team meetings (MDTs) to use a SF model and that this would leave teams (i.e., teachers, special education technicians, attendants, consultants, counselors, and administrators) feeling lighter and more hopeful, with an action plan for the student we discussed.

From there, we expanded the approach to classroom-based practices led by the teachers and special education staff who were early adopters. We felt that we could let the momentum provide the impetus for further change. We brainstormed, first as a leadership team and then as a whole staff, about all the processes that could be reimagined through a SF lens while only committing to the first step in the process as an entire team. This laid the groundwork for staff to move at their own pace to re-examine their practice and incorporate SF strategies and mindsets in their work. We planned ahead to incorporate SF strategies and tools as their thinking evolved. Box 8.1 illustrates the steps we identified as important to the initiative. We were very fortunate to have access to an SF consultant, as this provided scaffolding that allowed us to build on early successes and explore other avenues more quickly than if we had proceeded alone.

Box 8.1 Chapter Tips for Laying the Groundwork

- Identify how this change would benefit staff and students and decide how to start small and measure progress.
- Identify and support early adopters to create momentum.
- Brainstorm possibilities but ask for commitment only on the first step.
- Seek guidance from an SF expert, if possible.

Multidisciplinary Team Meetings

We believe starting with MDTs contributed to the success of the project because we were able to introduce the approach in a controlled setting that provided immediate, positive results. The school counselor, who had been trained in SF brief therapy, provided a rudimentary explanation of the rationale and asked permission from the staff to "try something new." No other training was required.

The SF trainer facilitated the first four solution-focused multidisciplinary team meetings (SF MDTs) which offered a few advantages. We believed teachers may have been more open to trying something new in the presence of a guest. Also, since the trainer had little or no prior information about the student or the problem, she focused exclusively on the process, which provided a more faithful SF model. Finally, these meetings functioned as informal and effective training sessions for the school counselor and principal, who were able to take over the facilitation role soon afterward. The school counselor continued to hold SF MDTs for the remainder of the school year. The principal, school counselor, and staff agreed that they did not want to return to traditional meetings. We believe the way the SF model was introduced and supported was key to this success. The school counselor sums up what worked:

> A selling point is that meetings are much more productive, even with some hesitancy at first, because you always leave with something, whereas before, I felt like we were just venting. With the SF meeting, you can get to solutions and strategies much faster.... The way we used to do it was heavy. You leave with such a heavy, negative feeling that taints the whole day. So it's important to leave us feeling hopeful and optimistic that we can do something, even if it's one thing.

Creating Successful Solution-Focused Multidisciplinary Teams

From our experience, we can suggest that launching successful SF MDTs without prior training can be simple. At the beginning of the meeting, the facilitator can ask for permission to try something new:

> Before we start, I would like to ask if you would be willing to try something new. We usually spend a lot of time in these meetings going over all the details of the problem, and we don't have time to do much else. We wrap up without any clear solutions, and we all feel discouraged. I have a new agenda to propose that might help with that. If we follow it, we are more likely to come up with solutions and might even leave feeling lighter. Would you be willing to give it a try? [If the group agrees, continue.] Okay. So it will be my job to ensure we follow this new agenda. If I see that we are getting off track, I will stop and redirect the conversation. Are you okay with that?

Once permission has been granted, a facilitator guides the meeting through an SF process. The trainer developed an SF meeting guide (Casey, 2023) shown in Box 8.2 with generic language so that it would remain accessible to those who do not have SF training. Whatever model is chosen, it is essential to follow an established SF structure to avoid falling into old patterns of venting and problem-saturated discussions. This means being willing to interrupt and redirect the group. Additional SF training for the meeting facilitator is helpful, but the meeting tool provides the basics for those who do not have it. We strongly recommend that the facilitator focus on directing the discussion rather than participating directly and ask someone else to take notes. Once team members have been through a few meetings, they are reassured that their concerns will be heard and that there will be a solution at the end. The staff quickly adopted the SF mindset and came to each meeting prepared for an SF conversation.

The following is the model we used.

Describe the Student

- First meeting: Describe three qualities or strengths of the student
- Follow-up meetings: Share the student's progress since the last meeting

The opening discussion is critical to the success of an SF meeting. If the facilitator allows the group to start with a description of the problem, it will not be easy to bring them back to building solutions without making them feel that their concerns are dismissed. Usually, it is enough to reassure participants that they will be talking about the problem in the next step and to gently remind them that they agreed to try something new. When we asked for strengths and qualities, meeting participants were able to generate a comprehensive list, even for the students they found most difficult to work with. If the group has trouble getting started, asking about the student's interests and activities in and out of school can be helpful, as they are a good source of strengths and qualities. The facilitator can make the link by asking, "What kind of skills or qualities does it take to participate in this activity?" or "What does this tell us about the student?"

Set a Goal [i.e., Preferred Future]

- What change would we like to see from this student?
- What signs or actions will tell us that this change has happened for the student?

It is essential to frame the goal as the presence of a positive behavior and not the absence of a negative one. The facilitator should ask the group to think about what they want the student to start doing rather than stop doing. When the group returns to the "stop" behaviors, we ask, "Suppose they stopped doing that. What would they be doing instead?" We also ask teams to provide a concrete description of the behavior rather than vague statements like "the student will learn to self-regulate." This is more difficult than it seems. We have used Dr. Ben Furman's (n.d.) video question to help teams formulate concrete descriptions: "Suppose you wanted to make a video of the student self-regulating. What would you tell them to do?" Although it may seem counterintuitive, it is not particularly important in this section to ensure that the goal is realistic. This work is done in the next section with scale questions. Sometimes, the discussion veers off into planning rather than describing the goal behavior (e.g., "We will add more time with the behavioral technician"). When this happens, we redirect the conversation by asking, "Suppose we did this, and it was helpful. What would we see the student doing that would tell us that it was helpful?"

Build on What's Strong [Scaling and Successful Past]
- On a scale of 1 to 10, where is the student now?
- What would +1 on the scale in the future look like?
- What is the highest the student has been on this scale?
- What was the student doing then that worked to make it to that point on the scale? What was the staff doing?

Scaling questions are used to generate hope and to ensure that goals and plans are realistic. We ask the teams to identify where the student is on a scale of 1 to 10 with the goal established in step 2 (i.e., preferred future). It can be helpful to define 1 in a way that suggests that no matter how bad things are, they could be worse, e.g., "1 means it is so bad that the student cannot come to our school at all." Scaling is also a quick and respectful way to redirect participants with unrealistic expectations. Once a team has determined that a student is at 2, it becomes clear that we cannot expect them to get to an 8 in the short term.

It is important to reassure the team that they do not have to agree on a number. Scaling questions are a language for talking about change, not a formal assessment tool. The facilitator can ask the group to agree on one number or the other or use an average. We have found it helpful to reassure the participants that they do not have to change their numbers. They can silently substitute their numbers when they are participating in the discussion. Once a number has been agreed on, we ask the team to carefully define a realistic preferred future, "today + 1." Again, we ask for a detailed and concrete preferred future, with follow-up questions like, "What will we see them doing? If this happened, what would tell us that it was happening? If we wanted to film it, what would we ask the student to do?"

Describe the Successful Past

Once the preferred future is clearly defined, we discuss the successful past. By asking what the student and the staff had done in the past when the student was higher on the scale, we identify strategies that are more likely to be effective and realistic. Again, this generates hope. It is important to encourage the teams to consider partial or temporary solutions and discuss them in detail. With enough detail about what has worked in the past, we can usually find at least one strategy that can be applied in the present. We also look for information about success in different contexts, in and out of school. With enough details, we may find strategies that can be imported from other contexts. For example, a student may function better in gym class than in math. If we have enough details about how gym class is different (e.g., the student feels more confident, the rules are clearer, there are opportunities to move around, and the student is part of a team), we can develop strategies that can be applied in other subjects.

Plan

- One or two things to repeat or continue.
- One thing the student can amplify or learn that is built on what they can already do.
- Who will help the student? What will each person do, based on successful past descriptions?
- How will we recognize, celebrate, and communicate progress with the student? Who will communicate with parents or guardians?

We start the planning phase with things the students and staff can repeat or continue rather than with what they need to learn or change. SF practice focuses on existing skills and strengths because it is based on the belief that students already have some solution behaviors and that we can achieve better results more quickly by starting with what they already know. One of the principal tenets of the SF approach is that small changes lead to bigger changes, so we are confident that building on prior success will have an impact. That said, we also assume that students need to learn new skills and behaviors, either because their challenges and difficulties are severe or simply because they have less life experience than adults. So, the planning stage also involves identifying what they need to learn. This part of the process is influenced by Dr. Ben Furman's (2004) Kids'Skills program, where behavioral issues are framed as skills to learn rather than problems to solve. It is important to take the time to identify who will be responsible for each aspect of the plan, to establish a timeline for the follow-up, and to specify how the team will communicate and celebrate progress along the way, especially with parents and guardians.

> **Box 8.2 Chapter Tips for SF Meetings**
>
> - Meetings can provide an entry point for larger SF projects.
> - Explain the benefits and get permission to try something new.
> - Assign a facilitator who can focus on the process rather than the content.
> - Assign a separate recorder to take notes.
> - Get concrete, detailed descriptions of goal behavior and past successes.
> - Focus on what has already worked in the past and tie new learning to what the student can already do.
> - Finish the meeting with a clear plan that identifies who will do what and a timeline.
> - Communicate progress with parents, guardians, and all stakeholders.

SF Training Applications Throughout the School: A Mindset, Not a Program

When designing an SF training program for a school, it makes sense to study the successes of leaders in the field, such as the Gonzalo Garza Independence High School in Texas (discussed in the following chapter) or the School of Merit in South Africa. These SF schools provide inspiration and are generous in sharing ideas and material. However, they also have training conditions that most regular schools cannot hope to provide. Budget constraints and substitute teacher shortages can make it difficult to release staff for training, and principal turnover can make it difficult to plan large-scale or long-term SF projects. However, we found that we did not need large-scale or long-term projects to have a meaningful impact on a school. The power of the SF approach is that it is a mindset, not a program. When staff learn how to think about problems and solutions differently, they often tell us that whether the project continues or not, they will never go back to looking at problems in the same way again.

The school team quickly adopted SF language and principles, perhaps because the approach reflected what they already believed about their students. As is often the case with caring teams who work with students who have diagnoses and disabilities, their attitudes were already strength-focused, but the structure and tools provided by the school system were not. In the training program, we set out to provide SF tools for classroom and behavior management that would be more coherent with their attitudes and values. We worked on expanding their ability to analyze problems through an SF lens, i.e., focusing on the preferred future and the successful past rather than on the origin of problems, diagnoses, and deficits. See Box 8.3 for tips for training that we used.

We had a total of 21 hours of training. We offered separate workshops for teachers and support staff to target specific needs, as well as combined sessions where they could work together. Throughout the process, the principal received informal individual coaching from the SF trainer. Our training workshops contained the following components:

- Introduction to the SF approach: origins, principles, the self-fulfilling prophecy, problem-solving vs. solution-building
- SF conversations about the preferred future
- SF conversations about the successful past
- SF classroom agreements used for classroom management
- SF reflections (for students who have had behavior problems)
- SF feedback for students and teachers
- SF skills building in individual interventions with students
- Planning time for teachers and support staff

> **Box 8.3 Chapter Tips for Training**
>
> - Present the SF approach as a mindset rather than a program to be followed.
> - Start with separate, tailored training for support staff and teachers and then offer combined sessions where they can work together.
> - Include time for teachers and support staff to plan how they will implement the SF approach in their classrooms.

In the introduction to this chapter, we made it clear that the SF approach is a mindset rather than a program since teachers and support staff are often skeptical of new programs. If we had not made this explicit, they might have seen the SF approach as just another in a long line of programs that would be replaced with something else next year. In our experience, this belief can be reinforced when we have limited training time and follow-up coaching. Regardless of the amount of training and the longevity of an SF project, we hope that once school teams have experience with an SF mindset, they will not want to return to a traditional problem-saturated approach.

SF Classroom Agreements and Management

Of all the training topics, the SF classroom agreement (Casey, 2022a; see Box 8.5 at end of chapter) had the most significant impact on practice. A SF classroom agreement is based on the idea that the classroom is a community and that all members of the community—not just the teacher and staff—are responsible for how it functions. Essentially, it is a set of rules and expectations identified by students rather than imposed by the teacher. The standard process is to ask students to imagine their preferred future and to use their answers to create a list of rules that reflect the kind of environment they want to have in the classroom. Teachers then watch for moments when students are following the agreement and reinforce good behavior by complimenting them and helping them identify the skills they are using. When problems emerge, teachers use the agreement to bring students back to the behavior they said they wanted to see in the group (Casey, 2022b). Examples of tips to use are below in Box 8.4.

Since our students usually need explicit instruction in social skills and group behavior, the teachers in this school were already devoting considerable time and energy to classroom management. Involving students in the process made sense to them, and they found ways to adapt the standard process to meet the needs of their students. Some groups required little modification to the proposed model. For example, students in the pre-work program had the communication skills they needed to brainstorm ideas for successful behavior in the classroom and their work placements. Teachers and support staff felt the classroom agreement reinforced the desired behavior, served as a visual reminder, and set the tone for a more successful school year.

In older groups of students who spent most of their time in work placement internships, the teachers captured the classroom agreements in written contracts signed by both teachers and students. This mimicked the contracts that students were asked to sign on work placement internships, in which some rules are imposed and inflexible (e.g., wearing steel-toed boots on factory floors) and some can be negotiated (e.g., more frequent, shorter breaks for students with autism and high levels of social anxiety). When teachers wished to reinforce appropriate behavior or address areas of concern at work sites, the contract was more practical than a poster.

Other groups required more significant adaptations. One teacher whose students had minimal verbal communication had a series of pictograms she had been using to teach appropriate classroom behavior. Rather than simply teaching the targeted behaviors as usual, she presented several pictograms depicting appropriate classroom behaviors. She asked students to select which ones were most important to them. The pictograms chosen by the students (give space, be kind to everyone, hands and feet to yourself, ask first) were posted on the classroom wall, and students were asked to sign them to show their commitment to following these rules. Students were invited to act out the rules, and at daily classroom meetings, they could give a pictogram to the classmate they felt had best modeled the rule that day. Teachers and students became adept at pointing out successes and noticing students behaving according to expectations. Students naturally adjusted their behavior to mimic those around them who were receiving positive attention. The students surprised the team by generalizing these behaviors and making reference to the pictograms outside of their typical classroom environment. This generalization of the rules is particularly challenging for students with autism and moderate to severe intellectual disabilities and was a welcomed benefit.

In another group, the teacher and support staff presented lists of behaviors and asked students to agree on those they thought were appropriate and inappropriate for their group by classifying them as "expected" or "unexpected" (Kuypers, 2011). The staff used examples and demonstrations to make sure students understood each behavior. They then created a classroom agreement poster where the behaviors were grouped under an expected "thumbs-up" or an unexpected "thumbs-down" heading. If a student was struggling with a particular behavior, the teacher could detach the corresponding "thumbs-up" behavior from the magnetic poster and quietly place it on the student's desk, providing a discrete reminder to help them get back on track. In group discussions, the teacher could ask if their behavior was expected or unexpected and help them make a choice that would benefit them and the group. The classroom agreement created a SF language around behavior for the rest of the school year, with the terms "expected" and "unexpected" replacing "good" and "bad" (Kuypers, 2011). Students adopted this language when speaking to each other and the teacher.

In another classroom, students were accustomed to having weekly class meetings to discuss difficulties and resolve issues. In this group, the students had difficulties with social skills, and many conflicts arose due to frustrations with expressive and receptive communication. The teacher and special education worker selected 30 phrases that could represent rules for good classroom conduct. The class spent several lessons reading each phrase, acting it out, and coming to a common understanding of what it meant. After this initial activity, each student was asked to identify the five phrases they felt would create a classroom environment where they would feel safe and successful. The students then shared their choices and came to a consensus about the top ten rules for the class. At their weekly meetings, the class discussed how they did collectively in following these rules. At one point, a student suggested that, as a group, they had mastered the rule of showing respect to the speaker by listening quietly. The students decided that since they had mastered this rule, they could select one of the "runner-up" rules to start practicing. They demonstrated genuine enthusiasm for this change. The adults were surprised and pleased to see that their students had taken full ownership of their class rules. They reported fewer interpersonal conflicts between students and noted that when conflicts did arise, the rules were used as a basis to discuss expectations and settle differences.

What I (JH) found exciting as a school principal was that while the entire staff received the same training and documents, no two groups approached the classroom agreement in the same way. There was a rich dialogue between teachers and support staff as they decided how best to implement the process.

> **Box 8.4 Chapter Tips for SF Classroom Management**
>
> - Classroom agreements are a concrete way to expand SF capacity.
> - For students with intellectual disabilities and autism, the SF process may need to be adapted. Teachers and support staff are best placed to do this.
> - Adapted SF classroom agreements should retain the fundamental principles: student ownership of the classroom agreement, collective action to maintain a positive classroom environment, and noticing and celebrating success.

Early adopters shared how their students engaged with their classroom agreements, how they had a common framework and common language for discussing and reinforcing expectations, and how the students themselves were self-monitoring and making a concerted effort to live up to their commitments. This created a positive momentum. When discipline issues arose, as a school principal, I too could make use of these rules and ask students to reflect on their actions and identify strategies to resolve conflicts or look for examples of past successes to plan better choices in the future.

Conclusion

From a principal's perspective, the adoption of a SF mindset has been a success. The changes in our MDT structure and the way that staff and students co-create and plan for the classroom have been transformative. The staff collectively felt as though a weight had been lifted. The complex nature of our students' needs means that sometimes we will never fully understand the origins of certain behaviors. Focusing our energy on examples where students are not meeting our expectations leaves us feeling heavy and discouraged. A SF approach is freeing, allowing us to shift our attention to moments when things are working better and to mine these examples for strategies, we can apply to help students succeed.

It would be a dangerous oversimplification to suggest to educators that identifying and understanding the complex diagnoses and looking at the functions or frequency of maladaptive responses is never warranted. In fact, it is sometimes essential. The key difference has been using this information to identify behaviors that are within the student's control, so we can develop a plan *for* and *with* the student that allows them to take ownership of their learning and growth rather than to define the areas where they are failing and to use this as an excuse for lack of progress or simply for reporting purposes.

We hope that with a foundation in SF practice and a receptive staff, each team member will identify areas of their practice where they can shift to a SF mindset. For example, our special education technicians and workers have begun to explore a SF roadmap tool to help students resolve conflicts and avoid repeated behavior problems. Our school administration team is looking to use a SF model to work with parents in meetings about discipline and planning for student success, major transitions, and reintegration after out-of-class disciplinary interventions. The possibilities are endless, and each small step in the right direction provides momentum and inspiration to continue to make changes that promote increased student ownership in their learning and growth. We hope the work we have begun inspires you to look for places in your practice where you can capitalize on your team's expertise and desire to see their students succeed and create positive change.

Box 8.5 Classroom Agreement

Solution-Focused Classroom Agreement (Reproducible) (Casey, 2022a)

Start with a message that the group is larger than the problem	♦ What are your strengths as a group? ♦ What are your qualities? ♦ What are you good at?
Imagine the future	**Suppose this class was exactly how you wanted it to be.** ♦ What would it look like? ♦ How would we be treating each other? ♦ What would I see you doing? ♦ How would you be talking to each other? How would you be acting with each other? ♦ How would you be talking to me? How would you be acting with me? ♦ How would I be talking to you? How would I be acting with you?
Create and post the agreement	**Summary of classroom answers (3 or 4 items):** _____ _____ _____ _____
Ask students to scale their behavior	♦ On a scale of 1 to 10, where do we hope to be with this at the end of the term? 1 _____ 10

© Sharon Casey, 2024.

Sentence Stems (Reproducible)

Introducing the SF Approach
- *The SF approach is a different way of thinking about problems and coming up with solutions. It's not a program that we will apply, but a mindset. Our goal is to make a permanent change in how we work.* (introducing the approach)
- *SF practices will help us find small, practical solutions to problems that will make a real difference.* (introducing the approach)
- *I believe SF will give us tools that are a better match for our values and beliefs about students than traditional, problem-focused approaches.* (getting buy-in)
- *Although we are doing this for our students, you might find that using this approach contributes to your own well-being.* (getting buy-in)

MDTs

Introduction/facilitation
- *Before we start, I would like to ask if you would be willing to try something new. We usually spend a lot of time in these meetings going over all the details of the problem, and we don't have time to do much else. We wrap up without any clear solutions, and we all feel discouraged. I have a new agenda to propose that might help with that. If we follow it, we are more likely to come up with solutions and might even leave feeling a bit lighter. Would you be willing to give it a try?* (Wait for response.)
- *Okay. So it will be my job to ensure we follow this new agenda. If I see that we are getting off track, I will stop and redirect the conversation. Are you okay with that?* (introducing the SF MDT and getting buy-in)
- *I'm going to jump in here. We agreed that I would redirect when we start to go off track. That's bound to happen when we are trying something new. Can we get back to ___?* (redirecting problem-focused conversations)

Describing the student
- *What are some of this student's strengths or qualities? What do you admire in this student? When this student is at their best, what do you notice about them?* (first meeting)
- *What are this student's activities or interests? What kind of skills or qualities does it take to participate in this activity? What does this tell you about the student?* (first meeting)
- *What signs of progress have you seen in this student since our last meeting? What efforts have you noticed from them? What have they been doing to keep things from getting worse?* (subsequent meetings)

Set goals/preferred future
- *What change would you like to see from this student? What signs or actions will tell us that this change has happened for the student?* (preferred future/goal setting)
- *What will we see them doing? If this happened, what would tell us that it was happening?* (getting a concrete description)
- *Suppose they stopped ___. What would they be doing instead?* (redirecting when meeting participants respond with a behavior they want the student to stop)
- *Suppose you wanted to make a video of the student doing this. What would you tell them to do?* (getting a concrete description)
- *Suppose we did this and it was helpful. What would we see the student doing that would tell us that it was helpful?* (redirecting when participants respond with a plan rather than a description of the preferred future)

Scaling
- *On a scale of 1 to 10, where 1 means the problem is so bad that___* [impossible answer, e.g., the student can't even come to school], *where is the student now?* (eliciting an answer that is higher than 1)

- *What would the next number on the scale look like?* (establishing a realistic goal)
- *"If they were at this number on the scale, what would we see them doing? If this happened, what would tell us that it was happening? If we wanted to film it, what would we ask the student to do?"* (getting a concrete description of the goal)
- *What is the highest the student has been on this scale?* (identifying instances of success)
- *What was the student doing then that worked to make it to that point on the scale? What was the staff doing?* (getting details of past successes)

Plan

- *What actions can the student repeat or continue? What actions can the staff repeat or continue?* (identifying a realistic first step)
- *What actions can the student amplify or learn that are already happening, even a little?* (identifying opportunities to build skills)
- *Who will help the student? What will each person do?* (building accountability)
- *How will we recognize, celebrate, and communicate progress with the student? Who will communicate with parents or guardians?* (fostering collaboration)

Classroom Agreement

- *I see what a good job you are doing with ___ [refer to the poster and give examples].* (drawing attention to positive behavior)
- *In our classroom agreement, you said it was important that ___. You have been working really hard on this and it shows. I have seen you ___.* (identifying instances of past success)
- *In the last few days, I have been really impressed with how you ___ [refer to the poster and give examples]. How have you been managing to do this?* (identifying instances and details of past success)

- *"One of the things you said you wanted in this class is ___. On a scale of 1 to 10, how are we doing with that today? What can we do right now to bring this up to a ___?"* (using the agreement to deal with problems)
- *"Our classroom agreement says that we want ___. We seem to be having some trouble with this today. What do we need to do together to get back on track? How can I help?"* (using the agreement to deal with problems)

Chapter Tips for Administrators

- **Focus on the process, not the product.** The idea is to create a community where students share responsibility for what happens in the classroom.
- **SF classroom agreements work because the rules are negotiated with students** (i.e., the rules are theirs, not yours).
- **Trust your students.** They want the same things you do.
- **Be curious.** Take time to ask probing questions. Get concrete examples.
- **Have a sense of humor.** If students name things that are impossible, laugh along with them and simply ask, "What else?"
- **Use their words and their ideas.** Resist the urge to interpret or reframe their responses. For this to work, it has to be their preferred future. If they sense that you are trying to steer their answers, they will not participate in the same way and the agreement won't work in the same way. Don't worry if some of their ideas seem redundant or they don't cover all the bases. Again, the process is more important than the product.
- Summarize **their preferred future.** Conserve their language as much as you can. Combine similar answers to form a short list of rules. When there are problems

and you have to get the class back on track, you will be reminding them of what **they** said they wanted.
- **For young students, act it out.** Create a game where they demonstrate the behaviors they want to see in the future. Only practice the desired behaviors.
- **Negotiate the answers to the scale questions.** Your answers count too, but the final numbers should be a group decision.
- **Post your classroom agreement.** Create a permanent document you can refer to (poster, etc.) when the class needs a reminder.
- **Use the agreement to deal with problems as they arise.** The idea is that they are a community, and they too are responsible for what's happening in class. Refer back to the agreement. For example: *"One of the things you said you wanted in this class is ___. On a scale of 1 to 10, how are we doing with that today? What can we do right now to bring this up to a ___?"*
- **Watch for success in the days following the agreement.** Take time to point out success and praise students. This will make it easier to get back on track when problems occur.

References

Casey, S. (2022a). Solution-focused classroom agreements. Available at https://www.lavoiesolutions.com/english/

Casey, S. (2022b). Solution-focused classroom management. Available at https://www.lavoiesolutions.com/english/

Casey, S. (2023). Solution-focused meeting guide. Available at https://www.lavoiesolutions.com/english/

Furman, B. (n.d.). *Kids'Skills for professionals training*. https://www.kidsskillsacademy.com/course/ben-furman-kidsskills-for-professionals-3-cr/

Furman, B. (2004). Kids'Skills: Playful and practical solution-finding with children. St. Luke's Innovative Resources.

Kuypers, L. (2011). The zones of regulation®. Think Social Publishing.

9

Involving Students and Families in Solution Building

Tara Gretton and Edwin Choy

Empowerment...is not something you give me, or I give you; we co-construct it between us by the actions that each of us takes.

Jackson and McKergow (2006)

In the previous chapter, you were presented with an exemplar of a solution-focused school in central Texas. This chapter provides two additional examples of solution-focused programs in other countries, where both focus on the stakeholders of students and their families. Specifically, readers will hear from Tara Gretton, a solution-focused practitioner and social worker based in Bath, UK, who discusses her experience supporting administrators, students, and caregivers in implementing the solution-focused approach across an entire school, a central component of a new strategy to enhance mental health and overall well-being for all students. Readers will also learn how Edwin Choy, a certified solution-focused therapist based in Singapore, has successfully worked with parents for many years, implementing a program involving parents in applying the solution-focused approach in their everyday lives in conjunction with schools. He emphasizes the importance of involving parents in the application and implementation processes, ensuring they are integral to the educational and developmental journey of their children. Edwin's program has shown that when parents are actively engaged and understand the principles and practices of the solution-focused approach, the outcomes for students are significantly enhanced.

This chapter provides practical examples for administrators aiming to implement solution-focused approaches in their schools. By actively involving all stakeholders (in particular students and parents), maintaining a focus on preferred futures, and ensuring sustainable practices, administrators can effectively enhance the mental health and overall well-being of their student populations, while also enabling the students to leave school with the strengths and capabilities needed to transition into the next stage of their journey in life.

Bringing School Administrators, Staff, and Students Alongside Each Other

In today's rapidly evolving educational landscape, it's clear that traditional methods are finding it harder to engage the current generation of students. Young people often feel disconnected from their school communities, left out of crucial conversations, and misunderstood. This disconnect highlights a pressing need for innovative approaches to unite school communities, co-constructing environments where every student feels included, heard, and understood. Susan Pinker, in her thought-provoking book *The Village Effect: How Face-to-Face Contact Can Make Us Healthier, Happier, and Smarter*, highlights the transformative power of community and collaborative thinking in education. She writes, "In education, returning to primal instincts of community and collaborative thinking can profoundly enhance learning outcomes. Through group projects, peer-to-peer teaching, and interactive discussions, educators can utilize the power of community to co-create a more enriching and fulfilling educational experience for learners."

Research supports the notion that we must move away from purely individualized approaches that focus solely on outcomes. Instead, we should prioritize connection, collaboration, and community, ensuring that inclusion and genuine accessibility are at the forefront of our educational practices. This paradigm shift calls for a break from the old mold and invites revolutionary thinking into our school communities. So, how do we catalyze this change? How can we work collaboratively across the entire school community, involving students, administrators, and staff in this transformative process? The answer lies in solution-focused thinking.

Envisioning a Solution-Focused School

Imagine a school environment where the focus is on what individuals do well and what they hope for. Picture a school community that collaborates to create meaningful change, where judgment is set aside in favor of genuine listening. In such a setting, students and staff are recognized as experts in their own lives, equipped with unique strengths and capabilities to achieve their envisioned futures, not only for themselves but also for their whole school community. This is the essence of the solution-focused approach. This approach prioritizes everyday interactions in a constructive manner. It does not pathologize or dwell on problems; rather, it acknowledges and empathizes with current challenges and gently shifts focus toward desired outcomes and existing successes.

The role of the school administrator in beginning implementation of the solution-focused approach is crucial to its success. Involving top systemic influencers in the school, such as teachers, counselors, parents, and even students can help to create buy-in as those persons see the benefits. In implementing the solution-focused approach in schools, administrators set the tone and vision of a solution-focused culture by modeling a focus on what is wanted and what is already working in the school.

The administrators can lead the way by training themselves in the solution-focused approach and supporting teachers and all school staff to train in the assumptions of the approach, encouraging them to take the approach not only into their everyday tiny interactions with the children and young people they work with but into their own lives as well. Additionally, administrators can allocate resources for professional development, ensuring that staff have the tools they need to implement solution-focused techniques and promote co-created practices among educators, students, and families. Through their leadership, administrators help establish a school culture that values constructive solution-building, co-empowers students, and celebrates small change, co-creating a supportive environment where all stakeholders can achieve their preferred future.

The Difference It Will Make

Implementing solution-focused thinking will fundamentally transform the school culture and overall climate, particularly by involving students in decision-making and training both parents and students in the approach:

- **Student Empowerment and Engagement**: Involving students in decision-making processes will co-empower them and give them a sense of ownership over their education and their well-being. This will lead to higher engagement levels, as students feel their opinions and ideas are valued and impactful.
- **Enhanced Solution-Building Skills**: Training students in solution-focused thinking will equip them with critical solution-building skills. They will learn to identify their strengths, set best hopes, and develop actionable small steps forward, while identifying and building on their unique capabilities and coping strategies, which will benefit not only their academic performance but also their personal development and overall well-being.

- **Stronger Parent-Student Relationships**: Training parents alongside students in the solution-focused approach will enhance communication and understanding within families. Parents will be better equipped to support their children's educational and well-being journey, adopting a more cohesive and supportive home environment.
- **Inclusive and Collaborative School Culture**: By prioritizing the involvement of students in decision-making, the school will cultivate a culture of inclusion and collaboration. This will create a more supportive and dynamic school environment where everyone feels invested in the community's success.
- **Improved Learning Outcomes**: As students become more engaged and empowered through involvement in decision-making and the acquisition of solution-building skills, their relationship with education will improve and they will feel valued and equal. A collaborative and supportive environment is conducive to better learning and well-being outcomes.
- **Positive School Climate**: The overall school climate will become more positive and welcoming. Issues such as bullying, absenteeism, and disengagement will decrease as students feel more connected and valued.

By embracing solution-focused thinking and prioritizing community, we can create a school culture that is not only more inclusive and supportive but also more effective in achieving educational well-being and preferred futures.

Creating Change Happens in Conversations

Contemporary research by Bavelas (2022) suggests that conversations are not mere transmissions from sender to receiver. Instead, they are co-constructed through dynamic interactional processes. This perspective highlights the reciprocal influence between conversation partners, where listening and responses shape the interaction. Conversations are co-constructed efforts, with both parties sharing responsibility for the outcomes.

This co-constructed view has profound implications for various sectors, including education. Traditional educational systems often operate within hierarchical frameworks where information is shared on a "need-to-know" basis, particularly concerning data protection and confidentiality and strategic decisions. Such structures can cause an environment of secrecy or exclusivity, where decisions are made by administrators with limited input from staff, students, or parents and caregivers. Even well-intentioned initiatives may falter if implemented without considering the perspectives of those impacted.

True inclusion in decision-making processes requires more than surface gestures; it requires genuine efforts to involve young people meaningfully. This involves not just informing them of decisions but also actively seeking their perspectives, valuing their input, and integrating them into the decision-making process. By fostering a collaborative and participatory approach, educational institutions can ensure that the voices and experiences of young people are respected, leading to more effective and inclusive outcomes. The interactional perspective on communication suggests that focusing on the dynamics of conversations can enhance our daily interactions and strengthen relationships. This insight can be applied to educational settings to facilitate change and co-create solutions where all stakeholders have an opportunity to contribute their visions for improvement.

Achieving Inclusion and Training in the Solution-Focused Approach

Implementing the solution-focused approach successfully requires a collective effort from the entire school community, including senior administrators, staff, students, and parents.

Inclusion in decision-making and training processes is crucial for effective implementation.

1. **Engaging Stakeholders**: Involve students and parents from the outset. This includes consulting them on what they aspire for the school, and what decisions should be made to begin achieving those aspirations. It also includes seeking their feedback and incorporating their perspectives into the planning and execution phases.
2. **Training and Development:** Provide comprehensive training for all stakeholders in the solution-focused approach. Ensure that students and parents not only are aware of the approach but are also equipped with the skills to apply it in their interactions. Practice the skills and consistently expect the stakeholders to use them. Use the solution-focused approach in meetings, referral situations, conflictual situations, and more.
3. **Creating Collaborative Spaces:** Co-create environments where open dialogue and collaborative solution-building are encouraged and expected. This can be facilitated through regular meetings, workshops, and feedback sessions where all voices are heard and valued. Invite students from all year groups to be ambassadors for the solution-focused approach.
4. **Continuous Improvement:** Encourage ongoing reflection and adjustment based on the feedback and experiences of students and parents to refine and enhance the approach. Ask "What are we doing that is working so far?" at the beginning of every meeting or conversation.

The solution-focused approach represents a shift toward a more inclusive and collaborative educational environment. By genuinely involving students and parents in decision-making and providing thorough training, schools can harness the full potential of this approach. The best hope is to create a school community where everyone works together to co-create positive change and build on what is working well already, respecting and valuing each individual's contributions and perspectives. Through this collective effort, educational establishments can achieve more effective and inclusive outcomes, ultimately creating a more supportive and empowered school environment.

Taking Up the Solution-Focused Paradigm Shift

In Bath and North East Somerset, a region in the South West of England with a population of around 90,000, a bespoke implementation of the solution-focused approach has been integrated into 12 schools. Among these, one school, Beechen Cliff School, has embraced this approach comprehensively over the past six years. The journey has seen progress, setbacks, and renewed efforts, reflecting the ongoing nature of this transformative process. Beechen Cliff is a large state school with a small boarding provision, situated in the center of Bath. The school has a mixed-gender fifth-grade class of 380, but it is a boys-only school for 930 students in grades 6–10 (converted to the U.S. school system). The school's vision is that its students go on to lead happy and healthy lives, thriving as individuals and making a positive contribution to society. Its core values of aspiration, compassion, independence, and respect genuinely underpin all that it does.

I (TG) have had the absolute privilege to have been working at Beechen Cliff School now for six years. During this time, I have witnessed firsthand the transformative journey the school has undertaken to integrate a solution-focused approach into its fabric. In 2018, Beechen Cliff School in Bath, UK, faced a surge in demand for mental health support. To address this need, the school embarked on an organic journey to integrate a solution-focused approach throughout their community. The text below will describe how this school emphasized the crucial role of student and parent involvement in the process.

Establishing the Foundation
Professional Training
The journey at Beechen Cliff School began with foundational training for staff, which laid the groundwork for broader integration. The school initiated the process with key figures like Susie Ingram, the 12th Grade Pastoral Manager, and James Oldham, a school administrator. They hired and consulted with the solution-focused counselor (TG) and trained key staff members in solution-focused techniques. This initial training focused on embedding the approach into their interactions with students and provided the skills needed to support its implementation. The training consisted of three one-and-a-half-hour sessions over a few months. Support was offered throughout and follow-up sessions were offered throughout the academic year to support the continued application of the approach. What people fed back from the training was that it was experiential. They reported that not only could they use it in their everyday interactions in the school environment, but that they could apply it in their self-talk and in their personal lives. This outcome was created on the training basis of them carrying out solution-focused conversations with each other and choosing a best hope that was about them in or outside of school was encouraged.

Organic Growth
As staff began to see the benefits of the approach, enthusiasm grew. This early success created a ripple effect, leading to further development and wider adoption throughout the school. What made the training so beneficial were its experiential elements. The staff were able to practice using the solution-focused approach with each other, which enabled them to have a personal experience that related not only to them as school staff but also to their everyday lives in and outside of schools.

Corridor Conversations
As the staff training evolved, it became apparent that the use of solution-focused tools in tiny interactions, such as in the

corridors, could further impact the general communication across the school. With a general focus on noticing what students were doing well and amplifying this, there was a noticeable shift in the general school climate, and situations were being de-escalated more quickly. For example, "I can hear that you are really angry. I have seen you manage situations like this well in the past. What can I do to support you to do that again?" and "What would be a small step forward to making this situation better?"

Inclusion

The students involved at the beginning of the implementation of the solution-focused approach were from a wide range of the school community. A few of the students were from our LGBTQ+ community. It feels important here to mention a past student Gaia Samson Reed, a trans-woman who was instrumental from the beginning and went on to sit on the school Board of Governors. She had a particular interest in inclusion, equality, and diversity. Their passion for inclusion informed a lot of our work in terms of how we ensured that we were reaching every person in our school community, making sure that we were open and honest about institutional racism and discrimination of marginalized groups. We worked and still work closely with external partner agencies alongside our students to ensure that we remain inclusive in our practices.

Gradual Expansion

Building on the initial training, the school has expanded the approach organically.

Student Training

Recognizing the potential of student leadership, Beechen Cliff School trains Sixth Form students in solution-focused principles. These students are instrumental in spreading the approach throughout the school, including training younger peers and leading initiatives.

Peer-to-Peer Mentoring

This student-led training not only reinforces the approach but also fosters a supportive student community that plays a significant role in the approach's expansion.

Applying Solution-Focused Ideas in Restorative Conversations

The implementation of solution-focused ideas to support restorative conversations has taken place and has had hugely beneficial outcomes. In a 1:1 solution-focused session, students will often refer to a breakdown in communication between themselves and a staff member. They are invited to share what their best hopes for change are and to think about what they might do differently to achieve their best hopes. What is also offered is an opportunity to have a supported conversation with the member of staff. Students and staff have the opportunity to share their best hopes for change about their interactions in the classroom, and they each share small changes that they can each make, while building on what they have noticed that has worked in the past between them. This practice has led to less punitive approaches being used to manage breakdowns in relationships between school staff and students. Students and staff are able to have calm, meaningful conversations because of the focus on hoped for change and on what has worked in the past in their interactions. The students are first asked if they would like this conversation to take place, and the conversations are supported by a neutral member of staff who is trained in the solution-focused approach. The feedback that comes from the students is that they understand the staff member better and that they have much better interactions with the staff member moving forward.

Integrating the Approach Across the School
Embedding Solution-Focused Practices

As the approach gained traction, Beechen Cliff School has worked to embed solution-focused practices into various aspects of school life.

Behavior Policies

The school revised its behavior policies to reflect solution-focused principles, emphasizing positive reinforcement and strength-based interventions, with an emphasis on how students have managed their behavior more positively in the past and what they would like to do better in the future. This systemic change supported a culture of encouragement and growth. An example of this is rather than detentions, the students are given a short form that they complete by the end of the day and return to the teacher. The questions are, "How have you managed situations like this better in the past?" and "What might you do differently next time?"

Daily Routines

Solution-focused questions and reflections were incorporated into daily routines, such as starting each day with questions that prompted students to reflect on their best hopes and successes, such as "What are your best hopes for this week?" and "What went well last week, that you will just do more of?" This integration helped normalize the approach and made it a regular part of school life.

Creating a Supportive Environment

Beechen Cliff School makes solution-focused principles visible throughout the school to reinforce their importance through the following:

- **Visual Cues.** Posters and notices promoting solution-focused thinking are placed around the school. Posters carry slogans such as "What are you pleased to notice about yourself today?" and "We all have strengths and capabilities that can be built on." These materials serve as constant reminders of the approach's principles and benefits.
- **Identifiable Support.** Staff and students trained in solution-focused techniques wear green lanyards to signal their availability for support, making it easier for students and staff to identify who could offer guidance.

♦ **Corridor Conversations.** Staff are encouraged to use solution-focused strategies in an ad hoc manner throughout the day, especially when it comes to correcting students. There is an emphasis on connecting before correcting, such as saying, "Good morning! Great to see you today arriving on time! What helped you to arrive on time today? ... Would it be ok if you tucked in your shirt?"

Fostering Student Leadership and Involvement
Co-Empowering Students

Student involvement has become a cornerstone of the solution-focused approach at Beechen Cliff School in the following ways:

♦ **Strategic Involvement.** Students are actively involved in shaping how the approach is integrated into various aspects of school life. Their input is sought in decisions related to the approach's implementation and development. Students attend strategy meetings and take the lead on particular areas, in particular seeking feedback from other students on the implementation of the solution-focused approach.
♦ **Student-Led Training.** Trained students take on roles as peer trainers, helping to teach their classmates about solution-focused practices. This peer-led training empowers students to become active contributors to the school's mental health support system.

Expanding Student Roles

Students play a pivotal role in further developing the solution-focused approach.

♦ **Leadership Opportunities.** Students lead solution-focused initiatives, such as organizing events and creating support groups. Their leadership not only enhances their skills but also reinforces the approach's presence throughout the school.

- **Feedback and Adaptation.** Students provide valuable feedback on the approach's effectiveness and areas for improvement. This feedback is gathered via the means of online forms. This feedback loop helps refine the approach and ensure it remains relevant and effective.

Engaging the Whole School Community
Involving Parents and Guardians
Beechen Cliff School has extended the solution-focused approach to parents and guardians, creating a cohesive support network.

Parent Training
Training sessions (online and in person) are offered to parents to help them understand and support the solution-focused approach at home. This alignment between home and school strengthens the approach's impact.

Community Engagement
The school promotes the approach within the broader community, sharing success stories and highlighting the positive effects on students, through a weekly school newsletter. This outreach helps build broader support for the initiative.

Celebrating Successes
Celebrating successes helps reinforce the value of the solution-focused approach.

- **Success Stories.** Success stories from students, staff, and parents are shared to highlight the approach's benefits and impact. These stories serve as powerful testimonials (in school assemblies) to inspire continued engagement. There are testimonial assemblies for each year group across the school. These celebrations promote connection across the year groups, with younger students reaching out to older students for support.

- **Recognition.** Individuals who have significantly contributed to the success of the approach are recognized and celebrated, reinforcing their efforts and encouraging ongoing commitment. Beechen Cliff delivers postcards to students complimenting them on an achievement or if they have inspired someone. Everyone in the school community has an opportunity to send a postcard (including parents).

Monitoring and Evaluation

Assessing Impact

Regular evaluation of the solution-focused approach ensures its continued effectiveness and relevance. Surveys, interviews, and other tools are used to gather feedback from students, staff, and parents. This feedback is analyzed to assess the approach's impact and identify areas for improvement. The insights gained from evaluations are used to make adjustments and improvements, ensuring that the approach remains effective and responsive to the needs of the school community.

Evolving Services

By 2024, the impact and success of the solution-focused approach led to requests from students and parents to further align school counseling services with these principles, advocating for the school's counseling services to be exclusively solution-focused. This request highlights the organic growth of the approach and reflects how student and parent feedback has guided the evolution of the school's support systems.

The Heart of Beechen Cliff School

Beechen Cliff School is characterized by its deep commitment to its students and community. The school's solution-focused journey began and continues with the proactive leadership of Susie Ingram, James Oldham, Andrew Davies, and Tim Markall, in collaboration with me (TG). What set this initiative apart was the collaborative spirit that defined its development. The openness of the administrators to work closely with students, parents, and caregivers ensured that the approach evolved in a way that truly reflected the hopes and needs of the school community. Their openness to promoting a collaborative approach was essential for the well-being of their staff, students, and community. They believed in the voice of young people.

The success of the solution-focused approach belongs to everyone involved. The integration of this approach is not just a top-down directive but an organic process driven by the collective efforts and insights of the entire school community. The heart of Beechen Cliff School beats with a commitment to seeing and nurturing the brilliance in each student, and its openness to collaboration has been key to this success. This collaborative approach applies a supportive, co-empowering environment where every member of the community contributes to and benefits from the shared preferred future of enhancing mental well-being and creating a positive school culture.

The Wider Community – The Ripple Effect (Parents)

To be effective in education, there is a need for schools to engage parents to be involved in their children's education. In this segment, I (EC) share some successful programs that have been created in Singapore schools to engage parents. In particular, I will be sharing the parent-teacher bonding sessions that built a collaborative relationship to support the children's growth. The solution-focused approach to education is a wonderful way to help students develop a growth mindset – to see possibilities in themselves and their future. This approach can be reinforced at home through parental involvement.

As parents notice the progress taking place in their children at school, schools may introduce simple solution-focused concepts and skills they can use at home with their children. One way to do that is to have short workshops for parents to share what the school is doing in solution-focused education and also the benefits observed in their students and encourage parents to partner with the school in educating and developing their children.

There is merit in doing this parental involvement training on a class-by-class basis as a follow-up to the parent-teacher bonding session described in the next segment. This all-of-school approach engages parents as collaborators of change.

Some of the simple solution-focused skills that parents can learn and employ at home in engaging their children are:

- Building on success – how parents can notice and compliment what their children have done well and celebrate their achievements.
- Hopeful conversations – to engage their children in conversations that focus on their past successes and imagine their best hopes for their future
- Growth in small steps – to build confidence in their children by helping them to imagine the small steps needed to achieve their best hopes.

What a nurturing environment it will be for students when they are engaged with the same positive solution-focused approach both in school and at home! It takes intentional efforts from both teachers and parents, but the outcome for students is worth all the effort. It will help schools be successful in delivering their core service in education.

Engaging Parents as Collaborators of Change – The Process

The Rationale
Some parents have such high expectations of their children's education that they often unfairly place the responsibility on teachers for their children's well-being at school. This often results in unhealthy parent-teacher relationships brought about by seemingly competing desired outcomes. One approach to help facilitate a bond between parents and teachers such that

they work collaboratively to foster a nurturing environment for their children at home and school is to have a solution-focused parent-teacher bonding workshop. Using the solution-focused approach as a common tool creates a common language and mindset for parents and teachers to begin speaking positively about each other, their children, and the school.

The Preparations

With the support of the principal, we put all class teachers involved through a 2-hour session on how to apply their solution-focused skills in the parent-teacher bonding session to generate a collaborative relationship with parents. Then we invite the parents to come to school for the bonding session on a class-by-class basis to meet up with the form teachers and subject teachers for their children's class. This way parents of the same class not only get to know the teachers but also bond with other parents.

The Bonding Session

Getting to Know You

We start off the session with a simple introduction activity so that parents and teachers can know each other. It is not uncommon for parents to be pleased to meet the parents of the friends of their own child in that class. In addition to introducing themselves, we give parents the following prompt: "one thing I appreciate about my child is..." This group sharing begins with the first positive descriptions of their children.

Begin with the End in Mind (Best Hopes and Future Perfect)

We then have the parents reflect on the following future perfect of their child in this class:

> Imagine it is the end of the school year. It has been a successful year for your child, for you and your child's teacher. You all have smiles on your faces. What has made it such a good year? Come up with as many things as you can!

Then parents and teachers take turns to share their best hopes for the class.

What Has Gone Well So Far? (Building on Success)
We asked each person to reflect on what has gone well so far. Teachers are then invited to share with the group first "what went well with the students in class" since the start of the school year. Parents feel good that their children are adjusting well at school. Then we ask each parent to share "what went well with their children" since the start of the school year. Focusing on what has gone well helps parents build on the successes their children have made. The impact positive descriptions had on the entire group of parents and teachers is palpable. You could see smiles on their faces.

Finally ... Circle Time (Next Steps)
In this final round of discussions, we have parents and teachers sit in a closer circle and have each person share what they are willing to do to make their best hopes for their children become a reality. We asked each teacher to be the first to share "What will teachers do to help your child have a good year in class?" Then we ask each parent to share "What will you as a parent do to support the teacher in helping your child have a good year in class?"

Feedback
Teachers in this parent-teacher bonding program shared that they had a positive start at school by building a good rapport between teachers and parents. They can communicate how they can support each other for the benefit of the children. As such, there is a positive partnership between parents and teachers to help the pupils feel good about school and be successful in school. Trust was fostered and it made communication throughout the year much easier. Likewise, parents gave feedback that they enjoyed the safe communication with the teachers in the session. They also mentioned that this bonding will contribute positively to the child's learning. Solution-focused conversations have brought

meaningful connections through a shared vision of both parents and teachers. Because everyone was engaged in looking at present and future positive dimensions of school life (as opposed to an unhealthy scrutiny of problems), the instruments of hopeful conversations embedded in the solutions-focused approach have brought positive outcomes.

Conclusion

As we draw this chapter to a close. We would invite you to take a moment to think about your best hopes for your school. Tara always comments that each school she has worked with in implementing the solution-focused approach has done it in a bespoke manner that fits with their collective unique vision for their school and comes from a place of building on what is working well already in the school. Edwin, with his program for parents, also invites administrators to think about what they might take from the program to apply to their unique setting. However, something that Edwin and Tara both feel passionately about and advocate for is the importance of involving students and parents. We hope from what has been shared with you that you too can see the power and collective impact that can be had from centralizing a collaborative community approach that genuinely involves all stakeholders. The solution-focused approach by its very nature sees each person as an expert in their own lives and from this belief comes collective conversations that can change the face of our education systems for the better.

Key Points of the Chapter
1. **Active Involvement of All Stakeholders**: The chapter highlights the importance of involving students, parents, and school staff in the implementation of the solution-focused approach. This collective engagement is really important for the success of mental health and well-being strategies in schools.

2. **Solution-Focused Conversations**: Both Tara and Edwin stress the importance of focusing on what is working in people's lives rather than problems. This approach supports students, parents, and staff to identify and build on existing strengths and unique capabilities.
3. **Sustainable Implementation**: The experiences shared in this chapter underline the need for a clear and sustainable implementation strategy. By involving all stakeholders and ensuring they understand and support the approach, schools can create a supportive environment that promotes mental health and well-being. Because this is ultimately about the lives of the students, they need to be central to any planning and decision-making.
4. **Early Intervention**: Tara's transition from social work to education highlights the importance of early intervention. By addressing issues before they reach a crisis point, schools can provide timely support to students and families. This can be enhanced by having a whole school approach, where solution-focused approaches are used across the school in everyday interactions, and by students and parents being involved at a strategic level.

Chapter Tips for Administrators (from Students Themselves)

Collaboration at every tiny step is key. Permission and choice are paramount. How often we ask permission of students in particular, and parents is considered important and respectful. The solution-focused approach allows us to gently seek permission and give space for choice in a beautiful manner.

Encourage Student Participation
- Involve Students in Planning: Include students in planning and decision-making processes, particularly those related to school culture and policies.

- Train Students in the Solution-Focused Approach. This training should be the same as the training the staff and parents receive.
- Student-Led Initiatives: Support and promote student-led initiatives that focus on applying a positive and caring school environment. Provide them with the resources and support they need to succeed.

Building Relationships
- Acknowledge Small Signs of What Is Working across the School and Individually: Make it a routine to notice and amplify small wins and improvements in students' behavior and performance. Praise should be specific and genuine.
- Create "Noticing" Rituals: Develop school-wide rituals for recognizing and celebrating positive actions. For example, a "Postcard System" where students and staff can post cards to each other of appreciation for others' achievements.

Actively Listen and Respond
- Hold Listening Sessions: Organize regular listening sessions where students can voice their ideas and concerns. Create a safe and open environment for sharing.
- Act on Feedback: Demonstrate that students' ideas and feedback are valued by taking visible actions based on their input. Communicate how their suggestions are being implemented.

Build Feedback Loops
- Create Feedback/feedforward Channels: Establish various channels for students to provide feedback, such as suggestion boxes, online forms, or designated office hours with staff, such as an invitation to staff meetings and meetings with governors.

- Provide Updates: Regularly update the school community on how feedback has been used to make changes or improvements. Recognize and thank those who provided input.

Support Growth and Development
- Offer Support Resources: Provide resources and support for students and staff to develop and build on their strengths. This could include mentorship programs, workshops, or additional training.
- Highlight Progress: Regularly highlight progress and improvements, no matter how minor. Share success stories and examples of how the solution-focused approach is making a difference.

Tips for Involving Parents
- Consider starting the year with parent-teacher bonding for the first-year students and then progressively add on another level the following year. This makes the transition manageable and hence ensures success. Parents can be informed at the onset when they enroll their children that the school has an all-of-school solution-focused education approach including parental involvement.
- Teachers can be prepared to engage the parents positively. Parents can be prepared, through training, to engage their children, with simple and immediately implementable solution-focused skills. This creates a nurturing culture where students, teachers, and parents can thrive.

References

Bavelas, J. B. (2022). *Face-to-face dialogue: Theory, research, and applications*. Oxford University Press.

Jackson, P. Z., & McKergow, M. (2006). *The solutions focus: making coaching & change SIMPLE*. John Murray Business.

Pinker, S. (2015). *The village effect: How face-to-face contact can make us healthier and happier*. Vintage Canada, Reprint edition.

10

Exemplar

Strategies to Get Started in Your School

Xiao Ding, Jeeyeon Hong, Cynthia Franklin, and Linda Webb

Unlike many other leadership roles in institutions and organizations, school administrators often find themselves echoing the famed soliloquy from Shakespeare's Hamlet: *To be, or not to be, that is the question*—especially after handling a dozen incidents reported by teachers, negotiating with irate parents over the phone regarding their distressed child, and contacting emergency medical services to activate the care plan for a student's seizure or injury, only to realize that it's merely halfway through the day. The daily hurdles and mounting responsibilities school administrators face are often invisible to the outside world. It's a role that's far from the spotlight, demanding quick adaptation to ever-changing duties while also juggling personal and family life. Therefore, steering your school toward a solution-focused school could serve as the most comprehensive and ultimate transformation for an administrator.

Having explored many key aspects of the solution-focused approach throughout this book, we now turn to this concluding chapter, where you can integrate what you have learned and explore strategies that you can use to get started in your school. In this chapter, we provide you with practical guidelines that have been successful at Garza Independence High School—an exemplar tier-one, solution-focused alternative high school. What we share here are several examples from our experiences and research on the development of the solution-focused high school. You can read these additional resources about Garza to learn more about how to anchor solution-focused brief therapy (SFBT) in your school (Franklin & Guz, 2017; Franklin et al., 2012; Franklin et al., 2018). Our goal is to equip you with the lessons we have learned over the years, alongside actionable tips, that you may able to adapt to your school.

Preparing Yourself as a Solution-Focused Educator

> When I was a student, I never saw my administrators smile. In elementary school, my principal was infamous for knocking on classroom doors and calling kids into her office. They'd always return with red eyes and puffy cheeks. In middle school, our administrators were officers patrolling the halls, writing detention slips to any student who was in the hallway after the last bell rang. My high school principal was new to our school district, a white man leading a Black school and a Black staff, and he always seemed to be in a constant state of stress. I was sure of one thing: There was nothing joyous about being in school leadership.
>
> (Harris, 2022)

This clip came from an article featuring a former schoolteacher who transitioned into a role as an administrator, sharing his journey and the insights gained from his experiences with administrators during his own schooling and teaching career. Harris (2022) and I (XD), coming from different cultural backgrounds, find common ground in our experiences with administrators as both students and school staff. Perhaps, you recognize similarities between these experiences and what is going on at your school. You are ready to transform your school from a hierarchical structure to a more collaborative one by using solution-focused strategies. As an administrator, your role extends beyond managing. You are an educator committed to nurturing a solution-driven school system by performing significant administrative tasks. Thus, you are convinced that you can be more than just a crisis manager or a middle manager responding to higher-ups. Your role authorizes you the power to proactively include students and teachers in decision-making processes, fostering a culture where everyone's input is valued and can thrive. This type of vision prepares you to anchor your school in the solution-focused approach. As noted by Osborn et al. (2014), the successes of a change in a school environment hinge on the administrator's full support and active engagement, and your commitment to these core beliefs is the launching pad to getting started in your school.

Next, to get started you need to embrace and lead others in the school to learn the fundamental beliefs that anchor a solution-focused educational approach. These core tenets, rooted in hope, empowerment, and growth, should serve as the roadmap that directs your practices and shapes the procedures for cultivating a solution-focused school environment. The essential beliefs that constitute a solution-focused educational philosophy are as follows:

- ♦ A student's background and historical context should not determine their life trajectory.
- ♦ Challenges stemming from a student's family or community need not predefine their academic or professional achievements.
- ♦ The difficulties and obstacles students encounter are potential strengths to harness for growth and self-enhancement.

- We believe small constructive steps taken by any school participant can lead to major changes in life.
- We trust each individual within the school possesses capacities that can be nurtured to ensure successful outcomes.

(Adapted from *Our Educational Philosophy*, Gonzalo Garza High School, n.d.)

Learning this educational philosophy is a beginning, but to be totally effective in your school, you will need to practice and model to everyone these core perspectives.

Strategies to Get Started in Your School

After reading the chapters in this book, you are ready to initiate the solution-focused transformation process within your school guided by core beliefs. You may wonder, "Where do I begin?" Indeed, adopting a solution-focused structure in a school is not simply a matter of ticking a box. The integration of solution-focused principles—such as humanity, kindness, empathy, and a growth mindset—may seem daunting, and knowing where to start is challenging. To assist you, we suggest incorporating solution-focused coaching techniques to train yourself further and other staff and to scaffold the transformation with actionable daily solution-focused practices and reflections. Table 10.1 presents a selection of such practices that we have compiled from our experiences to help you take some meaningful first steps toward building a solution-focused school.

Establish Core Groups

If you stick to daily routines and are mindful of your solution-focused practices and philosophies, congratulations—you have already taken the difficult first step. Now, as a school administrator, you probably have recognized that creating a solution-focused school should never be a one-person job. It requires a team. If

TABLE 10.1

SF Practices and Presuppositions to Get Started

DAILY SF PRACTICES	ASSUMPTIONS
Keep an open-door policy	• Your teachers, staff, and students may need to see you a couple of times throughout the day • Your office is a safe and confidential space for conversations • You are willing and committed to support your staff and students during difficult days and times • You want to keep a close relationship with everyone at the school
Set up a morning greeting routine	• Personal interactions with you set a positive tone for the day for teachers, staff, and students • Staff and students need to feel recognized and supported to start their day • You value creating a sense of community and belonging • You are committed to embodying your solution-focused education philosophy through small actions
Daily SMART goals reflection (Specific, Measurable, Achievable, Realistic, Timely)	• Keeping your numerous administrative tasks specific and measurable will provide a sense of purpose and direction • Starting the day with a clear set of goals can lead to more proactive leadership and management • You need tangible tools to align the efforts of all stakeholders with the school's strategic plan
Staff and student spotlight	• Publicly recognizing individual strengths (such as through announcements) reinforces positive behaviors and motivates others to strive for similar recognition • Regular affirmations contribute to a positive school culture and enhance a sense of community • Efforts made by any school member toward positivity and change are valuable and worthy of notice

(Continued)

TABLE 10.1 (Continued)

DAILY SF PRACTICES	ASSUMPTIONS
Walk-throughs	• Administrators make themselves relevant to classrooms and students' daily lives by showing up • Observing classes helps you stay informed about the day-to-day teaching and learning • Regularly dropping by in a supportive and non-judgmental way reduces barriers between administrators, teachers, and students
End-of-day solution-focused note	• Trusting the process nurtures resilience and personal growth, even on challenging days • Writing down what happens each day helps you see how small steps are moving you toward your SMART goals • Use of positive notes helps maintain focus on strategic goals and bigger pictures amidst daily tasks. • Acknowledging your own successes can boost personal morale and readiness for the next day

you haven't done so yet, start identifying the champions of the solution-focused approach in your school. So, ask yourself: *Who are my team members?* The truth is you need advocates, representatives who are interested in or have already learned about SFBT. It will be an advantage for you to have a transdisciplinary team that will become your core group. Key to the formation of SFBT at Garza, for example, has been a group of teachers, counselors, and social workers who received professional development on SFBT and are now capable of providing coaching and training within the school. At Garza High, we also established a Student Service Team, which comprises cross-disciplinary stakeholders that work together on student success. Members of this team meet weekly and rotate over time to give others in the school a chance to lead. The solution-focused mindset is particularly conducive to transdisciplinary collaboration, as it emphasizes viewing others as experts, fostering openness to diverse ideas, and promoting mutual respect (Franklin et al., 2008). Feel free to invite your school mental health and administrative teams to join your core group. Gathering and sustaining groups of senior teachers committed to a solution-focused mindset is crucial. These teachers can advocate for the training of new staff, which is essential for long-term success (Franklin et al., 2018).

You will likely need several initial meetings with your core group to establish the group's rhythm and attributes. The first few meetings should include co-facilitated debriefings where you collaboratively develop a more formal meeting agenda with everyone present. De Jong and Berg (2012) extensively discuss the essential "not-knowing" stance in facilitating solution-focused conversations. To orient and open up the team, consider asking a few probing questions. Here are some effective examples from Franklin et al. (2018, p. 36):

What made you become a teacher?

What motivates you in this profession?

How can I help you remember why you became an educator?

What makes education work?

How can I support you so your students will succeed?

How can I help you change the world?

View these initial gatherings as collective brainstorming sessions to initiate plans and establish a routine meeting agenda. This marks the beginning of the solution-building process within your team. Further questions that can open conversations and tap into the team's strengths during these meetings include:

What do you appreciate most about yourself as a teacher?

What resources do you know that might help in this situation?

What strengths do you see in our team that can increase our success?

Creating a bond and trust during these initial discussions is crucial, as it helps leverage existing strengths toward a more solution-focused approach. Assign a group member to take notes for future reference. Additionally, ask a volunteer to draft specific steps discussed during these meetings, such as the frequency and timing of future group gatherings, regular participants, common goals or best hopes identified, and one solution-focused technique or philosophy to practice each week. These tasks will eventually contribute to a more formalized meeting agenda.

Continuous Professional Development and Supervision

Once you have identified the champions of SFBT in your school and established the core team, your next steps include coordinating ongoing professional development for teachers and staff and providing solution-focused supervision to facilitate continuous change. Collaborating with teaching staff to develop a shared vision through solution talks is crucial. Recognize that teachers bring a wealth of knowledge and experience from their daily interactions with students. By showing respect for teachers and promoting a collaborative environment, administrators build trust within the team. This trust leads to better care for students and creates a supportive atmosphere that allows them to feel valued and empowered to succeed. As a leader, initiating this positive cycle through focused relationship-building, fostering teamwork, and supporting all school community members is essential.

Solution-Focused Talks

Whether brief or extended, these conversations are essential for achieving our goals. Initiating solution-focused discussions is not difficult—you can begin with simple dialogues that highlight *what is working* among the teachers. We recommend two methods to facilitate deeper explorations in these solution talks to strengthen a solution-focused mindset and increase success.

The Miracle Scale

The first tool is the miracle scale, recommended by de Shazer et al. (2021) in their book *More Than Miracles*. This scale integrates the miracle question commonly used in SFBT. To apply it, you must first define what 0 and 10 represent for your teachers and team at a given time. We suggest setting 0 not as a point of powerlessness or the worst scenario but rather when teachers and staff feel the need to seek guidance. This interpretation of 0 helps you to ask follow-up questions that uncover strengths, such as *How have things not gotten worse?* or *What actions have kept you going before seeking help?* Conversely, a 10 on the scale represents the ideal outcome or miracle that the teacher or staff hopes to achieve. However, be mindful when exploring this ideal state, as many might move to the past tense in describing their hopes. The scale is a logical tool to identify elements of the desired outcome already occurring. Ask questions like *When was the last time you got what you desired with student A or parent B—even a little bit?* Continue to detail these instances and encourage staff to envision achieving the full miracle. For example, ask *What does one step higher look like from where you currently are?* This approach helps staff build a clear vision with actionable steps, enhancing their ability to implement changes immediately after leaving your office or a meeting.

Compliments and Self-Compliments

The second tool is the compliment. Compliments are indispensable in establishing trust and building rapport within a team. When an administrator extends a compliment, it effectively shifts the focus from problems to strengths, either directly or indirectly. Consider a scenario where a teacher, overwhelmed by a challenging situation with a student, seeks your support. Rather than calming her with mere words or delving deeper into the problem, a direct compliment such as, *Wow! I am really impressed by how much you cared for that student!* can instantaneously redirect her attention from the issue to her dedication and passion for teaching. This approach is likely to uplift and soothe the teacher more effectively than many words might. Following this, you could offer an indirect compliment, incorporating your personal observations of her strengths: *I was really impressed by how you handled that difficult situation in the classroom today. You managed to stick to your teaching material while still engaging with this particular student. How did you do it?* This inquiry not only emphasizes her control over the situation but also suggests that she possesses additional resources that helped her navigate the incident. Moreover, as a supportive leader, it is beneficial to promote and encourage staff to self-compliment. Seize any opportunity to foster self-appreciation (i.e., positive statements about themselves that are positive in nature) (Thomas, 2016); such compliments are often framed as "I" statements by staff: *I decided to bring this to our school mental health team and plan for the next steps for the student*, recounting their actions or knowledge. You might want to respond with: *You did the right thing by reaching out to professionals for support!* These affirmations serve as powerful reinforcements for positive changes and progress in discussions focused on solutions. For instance, if staff members report that parents have noticed their children enjoying school more that week, prompt them with, *Could it be that you are doing something right this week that contributed to his positive changes?* This encourages teachers and staff to engage in self-complimenting, which is crucial for cultivating both self-empathy and self-care among your team.

Provision of Resources and Training
Additionally, ensuring that everyone has the necessary resources, such as training, materials, and support networks, is pivotal for nurturing the continuity of a solution-focused school. Your ultimate goal is to have all staff members proficient in the solution-focused approach (Franklin et al., 2018). However, before achieving this, you need to approach the process with care and strategically plan the incremental increase of knowledge

in a practical and logical manner. Assess your baseline knowledge of the solution-focused approach and your budget to scale your efforts appropriately. Existing staff can take on roles as solution-focused advocates to facilitate training. Cultivating a solution-focused school is like planting a garden: the principal may provide the soil and the initial seeds, but it's the teachers or school staff who act as the gardeners, nurturing the seeds, watering them, and ensuring they grow into flourishing plants. Just as a garden thrives with the collaborative efforts of many, so does the solution-focused school flourish when every community member takes ownership and cultivates it. Below, we detail some strategies we have employed to sustain Garza, which we recommend for your consideration.

- **Brown Bag Sessions:** Hosting informal gatherings like Brown Bag Sessions during lunch provides staff with opportunities to engage in discussions, watch relevant videos, and share insights in a relaxed setting. These sessions can serve as valuable platforms for learning, role-plays, idea exchange, and professional development, fostering a culture of continuous improvement and collaboration among staff members (Kelly et al., 2008, p. 78).
- **Book Club:** Creating a space for a book club and providing a library of SFBT literature can encourage staff to engage in ongoing learning and discussion around key concepts and strategies (Kelly et al., 2008, p. 78).
- **Handout about SFBT:** Providing teachers and staff with a handout on SFBT techniques can be beneficial. This quick reference sheet offers easy access to key SFBT principles, strategies, and techniques, enabling educators to apply solution-focused practices effectively in their interactions with students (Kelly et al., 2008, p. 78).
- **In-Service Training:** Organizing training sessions for the entire staff allows everyone to receive structured guidance. This can be facilitated through small groups or

champions of SFBT sharing their experiences with others, fostering a peer-to-peer learning environment. Alternatively, external experts can conduct training sessions, followed by small group discussions led by SFBT leaders for further insights (Kelly et al., 2008, p. 78). Bringing insights from these smaller group discussions to larger meetings promotes broader engagement and involvement of stakeholders in the implementation of SFBT principles within the school community.

- **Guest Lecture:** Inviting experts or curriculum specialists to deliver training sessions offers valuable insights and perspectives to staff members. Administrators can participate as fellow learners rather than authoritarian or supervisor.
- **Continuous Training/Education:** Investing in continuous training and education opportunities, such as SFBT workshops led by social workers or external trainers, reinforces a commitment to ongoing learning and skill development. By providing access to specialized resources and expertise, schools can empower staff to stay current with best practices and enhance their support for students' social and emotional well-being.
- **Small Group Discussions:** Facilitating small group discussions throughout the week enables staff to reflect on their learning, share experiences, and identify areas for improvement collaboratively. This could be done in a more casual format, such as coffee and conversations.
- **Solution-Focused Coach on Site (optional):** Having a solution-focused coach on-site can significantly benefit a school by providing classroom consultations and modeling the solution-focused approach within the school environment (Kim et al., 2017, p. 63).
- **Hiring Value-Aligned Professionals:** First assess the school's staffing to determine if additional social workers, mental health professionals, or curriculum specialists

are needed to support students. During interviews, take a moment to delve into the candidates' mission and goals to gauge how well they resonate with solution-focused approach. This assessment ensures that new hires not only are qualified but also share the school's commitment to fostering a solution-focused environment (Franklin et al., 2018, p. 48).

Case Scenario

Your solution-focused team gathered for a Brown Bag Session during lunchtime. In this session, you explored a solution-focused coaching approach, discussing how ordinary words can be mapped onto a dialogic orientation quadrant to create new meanings and activate resources (Moon, 2021). Your primary goal for facilitating today's session is to enable your staff to reflect on their recent experiences with being solution-focused at school and to learn how to use the quadrant as a tool. Review the example dialogue provided below:

Administrator: Well folks, thanks for coming to our new series of brown bag sessions this semester. I appreciate you taking the time to join us and learn more about solution-focused approaches. Today, I plan to introduce something I recently discovered that I found inspiring—the solution-focused dialogic orientation quadrant. Before we start, may I ask what you hope to gain from our session today that may be helpful for you?

Teacher A: I've really been hitting rock bottom lately with one student, Faith, in my class. She just refuses to do her work whenever. I don't know, maybe she thinks my teaching isn't worth her time. I'm quite frustrated with this situation and unsure if I can continue being solution-focused with her because I really don't know where to start.

Counselor: I know who Teacher A is talking about. That student has been having a rough time lately and even missed Miss Kay's literature class—a class she never skips. As I'm still new to the approach, I'm open to whatever I can learn from this session. Any additional knowledge or skills would be helpful.

Administrator: So, Miss C, you're probably the only person here who learned SFBT in school before joining us. It's been a semester since we started working together. Could you share your best hopes for our time together this noon?

Social Worker (Miss C): Sure! I've been thinking about a few students on my client list recently, including the one Teacher A mentioned. I'm looking to engage more with their families to gain their support and help the kids function better at school. I'd be more than happy to learn anything that could help with that.

Administrator: Alright, let me quickly summarize our best hopes for today. Does focusing on anything solution-oriented that keeps us on track and better engaged with students and families sound like a good common goal? Would that be helpful for you?

Everyone: Yes, absolutely.

Administrator: Great, let's get started then [hands out copies of the book chapter]. I've been inspired by this chapter on how we can map our interactions with students. It uses a quadrant divided from past (on the left) to present (on the right) on the horizontal axis, and from negative (on the bottom) to positive content (on the top) on the vertical axis. Does that make sense?

Counselor: What does that look like in real life, exactly?

Teacher A: I noticed the diagram on page 252. It splits the timeline where the left represents the past and the right the future; however, all the lower quadrants are negative. The left is labeled "The Troubled Past" and the right "The Fearful Future."

Social Worker: Interesting, how can we apply this?

Administrator: Interestingly, the author mentioned that this quadrant should not be a questioning model but is intended as a listening model. It helps us orient a conversation to acknowledge students' troubled pasts and dreaded futures without delving deep. Instead, we use cues—ordinary words—to facilitate upward movement toward resource activation. An example from her podcast introduces the use of the ordinary word "instead." It involves a client discussing potential future challenges and current dissatisfactions. After listening, the author asked, "Clearly, you are clear of what you don't want. So, what do you want instead?"

Social Worker: Ah, I see, the exceptions.

Administrator: I think the author proposed some small words that can somehow be magical in practicing this shifting. I will forward you some YouTube videos that I found after this. But for now, let's practice using the word "instead." Can we give it a go, even if you did not do it perfectly?

Counselor: Well, I guess I could give it a go. Teacher A, you have seen Faith fail your class in many ways, so clearly you know what you do not want from her during your class. So, what do you want from her instead?

Teacher A: [Pauses and thinks] Well, I haven't actually thought about it in detail.

Social Worker: Suppose you got what you want from Faith, what might be the first small thing you've noticed that is different?

Teacher A: Well, I guess she would actually be looking into my eyes while speaking to me, and we would have a real conversation instead of brushing off each other.

Counselor: Wow, that sounds great. How would that make a difference for you?

Teacher A: At least we will have a real conversation and I can find out where to start to make my class more relevant for her.

Administrator: How else would that be different for you?

Teacher A: I guess I might come to find Miss C sooner and maybe plan together to reach out to Faith's mom to check in.
Administrator: Wow, all that sounds awesome.
Social Worker: I'd love to help.
Administrator: I would follow up with Miss C for another round of practice but we're out of our today's lunchtime. How about we continue to practice asking ourselves what do we want or know to do instead and finish watching the video that I shared?

[All agreed.]

Solution-Focused Staff Supervision: Step-by-Step

The steps outlined in this scenario are based on an actual Brown Bag session at Garza High School. The main difference is that, during that session, the first and third authors were invited as SFBT experts from a community-university partnership. Ideally, anyone in the group, whether they are outside guests, teachers, social workers, counselors, or other essential school professionals, can facilitate a session. However, if your school is new to the solution-focused approach, it may be beneficial to consider inviting external experts, either online or in-person, to lead initial sessions. This helps your staff model effective practices. Additionally, by inviting SFBT experts and trainees for professional development, you could potentially establish a long-term relationship with experienced trainers and attract potential employees who share the solution-focused values of your school.

No matter who the main facilitator is in a professional development or supervision session, it is crucial not only to absorb knowledge but also to listen carefully to your team members' concerns and thoughts. This active listening is essential for meeting them where they are with the solution-focused approach and for inspiring new learning opportunities that foster growth. The following steps, summarized by the acronym "EARS," which stands for elicit, amplify, reinforce, and start again (Turnell & Hopwood, 1994), can help you remember these key actions.

1. Elicit

Begin by checking in with your team members to understand where they currently stand with their students and the solution-focused approach. While you might enter a supervision or learning session with a specific goal in mind, it is crucial to actively listen to what your team most desires. Use this feedback to establish a common goal or best hope for today's session that will be most beneficial for all participants. To facilitate this active listening, the administrator posed a question after introduction, *"Before we start, may I ask what you hope to gain from our session today that may be helpful for you?"* This question is designed to recognize the concerns team members already have in mind before they arrive at the session. As this case takes place during the first gathering of a new semester, the administrator can also inquire in future sessions, *"What has been better since our last meeting?"* The purpose of starting group supervision with an *Elicit* phase is to immediately engage participants and encourage them to reflect on any positive developments.

2. Amplify

Once you have identified the positive changes, you need to inquire about the details of these changes while aiming to create a "Yes-set" along the way (Franklin et al., 2012). In solution-focused therapy, creating a "Yes-set"—seeking as many affirmative responses as possible during the course of solution-focused interviewing, whether verbal or non-verbal (e.g., nodding, maintaining open body posture, or expressing positivity through facial expressions such as smiling and making eye contact)—is essential for enhancing rapport and trust, increasing engagement, and reinforcing positive behaviors. In a supervisory context, creating a "Yes-set" helps to get everyone on board, fosters a sense of group cohesiveness and belonging, and supports the continuation of goal setting. An example from the case scenario is where the administrator amplifies the common best hope among group members by asking, *"Would that be helpful for you?"* The phrase *for you* is emphasized by both Lutz (2013) and de Shazer et al. (2021) as it validates participants' experiences, creates empathy, and fosters a personal relationship between the participant and the solution-focused approach. Another example involves clarifying details of the best hope by incorporating the participants' own words while amplifying these details. The counselor asked, "What does that look like in real life, exactly?" Similar questions like "What do you mean by 'general words the participants used (e.g., good, better life, nice conversation)'?" or "What does a nice conversation look like for you?" help in constructing the details of a desired outcome and in building steps toward realizing it.

3. Reinforce

Some reinforced solution-focused processes were also highlighted and are an integral part of solution-focused supervision. To reinforce is to ensure that team members participating in the supervision recognize and appreciate the positive differences. In the case scenario, the social worker has preexisting knowledge of SFBT. Many schools train their mental health professionals in common elements of psychotherapy models, which likely include core elements of SFBT. Taking advantage of such team members' expertise and encouraging them to co-facilitate or lead role-plays and discussions can be helpful.

Although leaving time for role-play may not be necessary for every supervision session, it can be crucial for a successful group learning session. Through role-play, team members can practice what they know while incorporating new SFBT knowledge or techniques being introduced. This enhances their understanding of how to use these techniques in their work at the school. For example, when the team practiced using the word "instead," the counselor directly applied the technique by posing a question to the teacher, successfully prompting the teacher to reflect on aspects she had not yet considered. The social worker, familiar with the approach, posed a miracle question to explore and reinforce the positive differences the desired outcome would make between the teacher and her student by asking, *"Suppose you got what you want from Faith, what might be the first small thing you've noticed that is different?"* After gaining more details of the desired status between the teacher and the student, both the counselor and the administrator continued to reinforce the positive difference by continuing the conversation with *"What else ... and how else..."* These types of questions may further the teacher's absorbing of the differences and envision the desired outcome she would like to see between she and her student.

In solution-focused supervision, it's important to allow conversations to flow organically while paying attention to reinforce any positive differences using these useful questions whenever appropriate. Reinforcement is typically accompanied by plenty of compliments. We have explained in a previous section how compliments and self-compliments can be useful and powerful in solution-focused talks. Here, the administrator also acknowledged all the efforts and progress made by team members with a direct compliment, "Wow, all that sounds awesome," to encourage them to take this learning experience into their daily work. Good closing remarks also gently nudge the practice and increase motivation to try different skills.

4. Start Again

Finally, the administrator suggests another round of practice with the social worker, focusing on her personal goal of engaging more with students' families. The administrator is preparing to initiate the *Elicit-Amplify-Reinforce* process once again. The key to successful supervision lies in continuously identifying changes, building a "Yes-set," exploring the details of the desired outcome, and amplifying positive differences to keep all team members engaged and committed to continuous learning and growth on the solution-focused track. Lastly, maintaining a transparent group supervision procedure is crucial, ensuring that expectations are clear and understood by all. Adapting the strategies discussed to align with your school's specific goals and learning objectives will also maximize their effectiveness and relevance.

Chapter Tips for Administrators

1. See yourself as a solution-focused educator who views difficulties and obstacles as potential opportunities to find strengths to harness for growth and self-enhancement.
2. Initiate change starting with yourself by adopting a list of solution-focused routines, such as maintaining an open-door policy, offering morning greetings, reflecting on daily S.M.A.R.T goals, spotlighting students and staff, conducting walk-throughs, and sending end-of-day positive notes. Never give up on a student.
3. Remember that it is essential to identify SFBT champions and formalize core groups to build and sustain a solution-focused school.
4. Pay attention to providing diverse training and resources to support continuous professional development and solution-focused supervision.
5. Utilize miracle scaling and compliments as the best tools to initiate solution-oriented discussions with your staff.
6. Follow the process of "EARS" (Elicit-Amplify-Reinforce-Start again) to facilitate successful solution-focused learning or supervision sessions.
7. Maintain a transparent group supervision procedure that everyone can easily follow and tailoring strategies to your school's specific conditions can maximize the effectiveness of building a solution-focused environment.

References

De Jong, P., & Berg, I. K. (2012). *Interviewing for solutions* (4th Ed.). Brooks Cole, p. 152.

de Shazer, S., Dolan, Y., Korman, H., Trepper, T., McCollum, E., & Berg, I. K. (2021). *More than miracles: The state of the art of solution-focused brief therapy*. Routledge.

Franklin, C., & Guz, S. (2017). SFBT within the tier 1 framework: Alternative schools adopting the SFBT model. In J. S. Kim, M. Kelly, & C. Franklin (Eds), *Solution-focused brief therapy in schools: A 360-degree view of research and practice* (2nd ed., pp. 73–98). Oxford University Press.

Franklin, C., Montgomery, K., Baldwin, V., & Webb, L. (2012). Research and development of a solution focused high school In C. Franklin, T. Trepper, E. McCollum, & W. Gingerich (Eds.), *Solution-focused brief therapy: A handbook of evidence-based practice* (pp. 371–389). Oxford University Press.

Franklin, C., Moore, K., & Hopson, L. (2008). Effectiveness of solution-focused brief therapy in a school setting. *Children & Schools, 30*(1), 15–26. https://doi.org/10.1093/cs/30.1.15

Franklin, C., Streeter, C. L., Webb, L., & Guz, S. (2018). *Solution focused brief therapy in alternative schools: Ensuring student success and preventing dropout* (1st ed.). Routledge. https://doi.org/10.4324/9781315186245

Harris, P. II (2022, November 4). *I never wanted to be a school administrator. Here's why I changed my mind*. EdSurge. https://www.edsurge.com/news/2022-11-04-i-never-wanted-to-be-a-school-administrator-here-s-why-i-changed-my-mind

Kelly, M. S., Kim, J. S., & Franklin, C. (2008). Garza: A solution-building high school. In *Solution-focused brief therapy in schools: A 360-degree view of research and practice* (pp. 73–98). Oxford University Press. https://doi.org/10.1093/acprof:oso/9780195366297.001.0001

Kim, J. S., Kelly, M. S., & Franklin, C. (2017). *Solution-focused brief therapy in schools: A 360-degree view of the research and practice principles* (2nd ed.). Oxford University Press.

Lutz, A. B. (2013). *Learning solution-focused therapy: An illustrated guide*. American Psychiatric Pub.

Moon, H. (2021). Coaching. Using ordinary words in extraordinary ways. In S. McNamee, M. M. Gergen, C. Camargo-Borges, & E. F. Rasera (Eds.), *The SAGE handbook of social constructionist practice* (pp. 246–257). Sage. https://doi.org/10.4135/9781529714326.n24

Osborn, R. N., Uhl-Bien, M., & Milosevic, I. (2014). The context and leadership. In D. V. Day (Ed.), *The Oxford handbook of leadership and organizations* (pp. 589–612). Oxford University Press.

Thomas, F. (2016). Complimenting in solution-focused brief therapy. *Journal of Solution Focused Practices*, 2(1), 3.

Turnell, A., & Hopwood, L. (1994). Solution-focused brief therapy. *Case Studies in Brief and Family Therapy*, 8(2), 39–51.

For Product Safety Concerns and Information please contact our EU
representative GPSR@taylorandfrancis.com
Taylor & Francis Verlag GmbH, Kaufingerstraße 24, 80331 München, Germany